T0198672

Out of the Darkness and into the Light

My Journey to Becoming a Medium

ALANA CLARK

BALBOA.
PRESS
A DIVISION OF HAY HOUSE

Copyright © 2017 Alana Clark.

All rights reserved. No part of this book may be used or reproduced by any means, graphic, electronic, or mechanical, including photocopying, recording, taping or by any information storage retrieval system without the written permission of the author except in the case of brief quotations embodied in critical articles and reviews.

Balboa Press books may be ordered through booksellers or by contacting:

Balboa Press
A Division of Hay House
1663 Liberty Drive
Bloomington, IN 47403
www.balboapress.com.au
1 (877) 407-4847

Because of the dynamic nature of the Internet, any web addresses or links contained in this book may have changed since publication and may no longer be valid. The views expressed in this work are solely those of the author and do not necessarily reflect the views of the publisher, and the publisher hereby disclaims any responsibility for them.

The author of this book does not dispense medical advice or prescribe the use of any technique as a form of treatment for physical, emotional, or medical problems without the advice of a physician, either directly or indirectly. The intent of the author is only to offer information of a general nature to help you in your quest for emotional and spiritual well-being. In the event you use any of the information in this book for yourself, which is your constitutional right, the author and the publisher assume no responsibility for your actions.

Any people depicted in stock imagery provided by Thinkstock are models, and such images are being used for illustrative purposes only. Certain stock imagery © Thinkstock.

Print information available on the last page.

ISBN: 978-1-5043-0824-3 (sc)
ISBN: 978-1-5043-0827-4 (e)

Balboa Press rev. date: 05/08/2017

ACKNOWLEDGEMENTS

To my wonderfully supportive family – My wonderful husband Leighton, my daughters Jessica, Kaylee, Tayler and Ella and my beautiful grand daughters Isobel and Indie, if it wasn't for you all and your support I could never have written this book

And to Erik Medhus, my Maternal Grandmother Carrie and my beautiful son's Neil and Matthew, who all helped me discover who I really was, may your spirits always guide and protect those who are discovering who they are and what they can do, without your help I would never have had the courage to pursue this path, I will love and cherish you all in this life and onto the next

CONTENTS

APPRECIATION

Being born "Awake" made my life very interesting growing up, as I never knew that the things I heard and saw weren't part of everybody's normal everyday life.

When I started to realise that not many other people actually saw the things I saw like the fairy we had in our backyard, it was then that I realised that I should keep quiet about those things, as people would look at me like I was crazy.

So when I finally bit the bullet and "Came out" to all my friends and family that I was a Medium and I was proud of it, I was really surprised that they didn't call me crazy.

It was a huge step for me as I saw the faces of some of the people I did tell years before and they looked at me like I had literally lost my mind they just went "oh" and then changed the subject.

So I wanted to say to those who stood by me no matter what their opinions were, thankyou.

I know most of you have your own opinions and truth and that is ok, everyone is entitled to their own opinion.

I would never just stop liking a person because they had different opinions to me, or if they were religious, or a witch, or whatever it may be, be proud of who you are, and let people come to their own truth in their own time and in their own way, you also can't force your opinions onto others either.

So the fact that all my friends and family just accepted who and what I was no questions asked makes me so proud of the people I have around me.

I want to thank the members of my facebook group Past Life

Memories and Discussions by Alana, without them in my life to support and to help me discuss topics that most people would think were crazy with love and support and no judgement.

I want to also thank my Medium Circle group, for getting together twice a week and discussing and talking to the spirits on the other side, and helping each other to be the best of our capabilities and beyond.

I especially want to thank my daughters and grand daughters for being there for me when I am tired and grumpy, and giving me cuddles or just helping out where you can, I truly appreciate it, and I love you all around the world and back again.

I want to also thank my step children, thankyou for accepting me as your evil step mother with grace and love, you have never given me a day of grief, you are all growing up such wonderful human beings.

Most of all I want to thank my husband who has grown with me in my journey, he didn't sign up for this when we married so he has been such a great sport. I love you very much, thankyou for choosing me.

I would like to also thank Valerie Jagenow for the beautiful book cover she designed

TESTIMONIALS

I had a wonderful reading with Alana, I sent her a picture of a possible contractor.

I lost my husband three years ago and after a long probate battle and ending up with much less money than I had expected, I wanted to make sure the contractor was a good fit.

When I had first met this man, I could have sworn there was an instant connection.

Alana included a past life peek into our lives together and found out quite a bit about who we were and what we had meant to each other back then, which resonated completely.

Alana also drew some Oracle cards for me too, and also included a message from my husband in spirit He said he was sending me some like minded people, as my solitary life has become very lonely.

My husband also said that he sent the contractor, and he will be sending more like minded people my way.

My spirit family is doing the same, I have been fortunate to be in contact with a few good people during my grieving process and depression.

Perhaps the biggest message was to always trust and follow my intuition.

My fear was that my intuition was feeling muddled and I was freaking out a bit.

This reading set me straight again and was a strong verification that my beloved spirit family is still paying attention, hearing and answering my prayers, and speaking through my intuition.

Also our loveable spirit friend Erik Medhus dropped by to confirm that I should go forward into my planned future, without fear, as long as I follow my intuition.

All is well and getting brighter.
Thank you Alana and team,
I love you all.
From Marge – America

I received a past life reading today form Alana, and it was mind blowing!

Not only was I given the names of my wife and children but I also got a sense of my personality (which really hasn't changed).

She went into so much detail, it was like I was peeking through a window in time, instead of reading an email.

My spirit message gave me chills and goosebumps, but most importantly, hope for the future.

Finishing with a past life oracle card which really helped me validate that I am on the right path.

I'm extremely happy with my reading and recommend to anyone with any interest in getting a reading to give her a try, you wont regret it.

Thankyou so much Alana, I really appreciate the time and effort you put into my reading.

From Crimzon Reaper – Canada

I had a past life reading with Alana, and she told me all about a past life of mine, which reading it made my heart race and my stomach clinched.

It was very detailed.

She also brought me messages from spirit of self love and how I need to work on it.

Feel first, think second – that was from Erik Medhus.

I highly recommend Alana, it was a fabulous experience.

From Jessica Cales Deacy – America

I must tell you about my reading from Alana.

I came to her today because I was suffering from what I thought was a serious issue.

I woke up at 5 am and I could feel something coming on, and I thought if this is a panic attack (because I'm an Empath) then I can work through it.

Well eight hours later nothing I'm doing is working, so desperate and thinking about going to urgent care, because I was starting to get scared, I reached out to Alana and told her what was going on.

I don't even know if I interrupted her day, but she got right on it for me.

She brought up a previous life with very, very specific information and told me that I had carried some feelings over in this life, including a sense of panic, feeling trapped.

I learned some more things about myself today and what I can do to better protect myself.

I highly recommend Alana, she is very very good, 5 stars all the way.

I also asked Alana to do a reading for my wife and I have got two words for Alana's readings: Holy shit!

I told my wife that in a previous lifetime that she was a nurse in a war – which was information I received from another Medium that my wife wasn't privy to.

Not only did Alana confirm that, but did she ever get in to the details, and then some.

My wife now understands why she has an affinity for medicine as she works in medicine today

Please please please, work with Alana, she is very very very good, Damn!!!

From Ryan Adragna – America

I had a past life reading with Alana, and it was a unique experience and now I know why I do certain things in my life.

I would definitely recommend a reading!

Thanks Alana you are great.

From Sheila Porreca – America

I had the honour of having a past life reading with Alana.

It was very enlightening and interesting to know a little more about the history of my soul's journey.

Truly recommend a reading with her, she is a very gifted soul.

Joe Gibson

I just had a reading with Alana and well I just have to tell you that she is amazing.

I chose to have a past life reading done and I was in awe the entire time I was reading it.

It resonated so much with me, past life reading's are not something I would not have chosen to do but I had a won a reading and decided to pick past life, although I hadn't thought it would be a way to find answers but I am here to tell you that Alana is so detailed with her reading and gives so much information it is well worth it to anyone!

Thank you again Alana.

Samantha Clark (no relation) – America

INTRODUCTION

Isn't it strange the way we just stare into space, or into the fire, or in my case the ocean as its right there in the view of my lounge room window and just think about life from the beginning, from the first day we remember life for ourselves, or just reflect upon things we have done, or that we have experienced.

It captures our attention out of nowhere and forces you to think about everything that has ever happened to you, the good, the bad and the ugly, I call this purging as I feel we need to remember these things so that we can let it go and move on, even though it can be really really difficult, I know. Why? Why do we need to feel the bad? Why can't we just feel the good?

These are the questions I asked myself over and over again, can time heal all wounds? Hmmm maybe some, but not all.

There are some things I remember fondly, and there are some that make my skin crawl.

The purpose of this book is to give you a little insight into what our lives, and my life is all about, from mine and spirits perspective at least.

Not everyone will grasp the concept, but I'm hoping many will see it from their own perspective, no matter what your beliefs are, you will see that what I talk about here is others perspectives on what happened to them and how they deal with it, or didn't, and how it changed them as a human being, I think any human can grasp that, don't you?

The rest of this book touches on my experiences and how I came to be a medium and how it changed my life, I don't profess to be perfect, I don't pretend I'm something I'm not, and I certainly don't make stuff up to appease the public, I am who I am, and I wouldn't change me for the world, I'm just doing what everyone else is doing, I'm trying to live my life the best way I know how, doing what I love, not what I have to do, and loving the fact that I have the support of my beautiful family in the process.

That is all we can ask for in this life, doing what we love, not what we have to, I do what I do because I want to help people discover who they are, who they were and who they can be.

If I have helped one person do that, then I have done my job as a woman, as a friend, as a wife, a mother and as a medium.

My life all open for the world to see... why you ask?

Well because there are many children and adults going through many things, that can easily be avoided if we just speak out, if we just work together and give people a chance, a chance to be who they are meant to be, a chance to recognise ourselves in someone and help, a chance to shine like we are meant to, a chance to see someone for who they are and have the strength to walk away if need be.

Most of all a chance to help to heal someone's past, by being present in their future.

Just by saying to someone, are you ok?, and actually mean it, can do wonders for someone, to actually care what they are going through and are willing to listen can literally save a life, so that's why I'm doing this, that's why I'm sharing my life to the world with no hold's barred, so I can hopefully change even just one person from living the "bad" that I had in my life.

My life is peaches compared to many others and I would never diminish someone else's experience as we all have our own demons to live with as such, but hopefully I can help at least one person from being alone, by being bullied, by helping them to master their own destiny, and to make a difference, so that's why I wrote this, I want the world to wake up, to see that what many people are doing is hurting, and most don't realise the impact they make with just a few short words, whether they are said in a way that is uplifting, or whether they are said to make someone feel smaller than they really are, our words make a difference, so this book is to show what words can do to people and how we can change that, and how we can be the master of our own destiny, and ways to get us there.

So sit back, get yourself a drink, a blanket and get really comfortable because this could take a while.

Love Alana

CHAPTER 1

Memories of my life

My very first memory I have is of me sitting on the hardwood floor in the house I shared with my parents and eventually my little brother 3 years or so later.

I was in the lounge room by myself while my mother was in the house somewhere, I remember thinking that the floor was very cold and I wanted my cat Mia.

I was around a year old, my parents had a photo of that day and I remembered it clearly as if it was yesterday.

I remember many other memories of my life between then and now but the following are the memories that have been stuck in my mind over the years The next memory I have that is clear as day was when I was 7 years old, I woke up screaming and crying when my father came into the room and tried to wake me up.

I was begging my father in my dream like state to let me go through the wall, and that they had promised I could go home, but now they said I couldn't.

The next morning, my father told me that when he was trying to wake me up, my eyes looked like I was staring right through him; he said it had freaked him out.

It was a very real experience for me, as I still felt homesick many days later, homesick for a place I didn't know and had never been to as far as I knew and it's something that has been in the back of my mind since then.

I know parents like to comfort their children and tell them it was just a nightmare and I know because I do the same when my girls have had nightmares too, because we don't want them to dwell on it, we want them to dream happy dreams, even when we know that it may not be possible, but we try because we love our children and I know for a fact I would do anything for my children for them to not feel bad, hurt, upset or anything like that that a nightmare may cause, so I could see where my father was coming from that night, but what I didn't tell my father, was that it wasn't a nightmare, in fact it had been my home, it was a portal to it and my real family was on the other side of it.

Sounds bizarre? Oh yes, for me it took years to figure out what it all meant and I will explain it all further into the book.

My next memory, I was asleep in bed one night when I was about thirteen years old, I woke up with strange thoughts in my head, I had this feeling that I would never get to wear a bra, get my period, get a boyfriend, drive a car, get married, have the four kids I wanted and finally just to move into a house of my own one day, I wanted to be on my own and not have to listen to my mother bang on my door while vaccuming on a Saturday morning at 6 am, and I had no idea where these thoughts came from, but I wondered if maybe it was a premonition or if I was just scared I would never get a chance to live them, but what I have learnt in my years of life is that a lot of girls feel this way, a lot of them think they will never get to experience these things because they feel so far away.

How amazing it was to me to finally do each of those things, as I felt as though I had never experienced them before, I think I had been dreaming about a life when I had died young, and I remembered never getting to experience any of those things.

There are times that I have wished my life had turned out differently, I wish I was rich and lived in a beautiful mansion and had a few holiday houses in different parts of the world, so that when I want the sun or snow I can just pack up and leave whenever I want, but like I said this is the real life of me, and those things are not in my future nor have ever been in my past.

To understand me, you need to know who I am and how I came to be.

My parents were both full time workers who worked hard, which gave us plenty of time on our own, and when we weren't at school we were at daycare, which although I wasn't that interested in as I got older, as I thought I could look after myself as I became a teenager but I made a lot of life long friends.

I grew up hearing voices in my head that I figured were just in my head, and that everyone could hear them too so I ignored them most of the time, I found they became easy to ignore as long as I was busy, I didn't have a lot of friends growing up so I spent a lot of my time alone, even at school and day care. Most of the time I would play with the younger kids because they would be innocent of drama, and I found drama to be very emotionally draining on me.

I had no idea at the time that I was an empath so when I got picked on or people were nasty to me, I would retreat into myself and hide away, if I only knew then what I know now I would never have let them dim my light, but it wasn't all bad I had a few shining lights in my life which helped me to become the strong independent woman I have become.

I was the first born child with my brother following three and half years later, and we really only had each other as we had grown up in Adelaide, South Australia, and our parents had immigrated from England a couple of years before my birth, so we had no Aunties, Uncles, Grandparents or any other extended family to talk to or be with as they were all living in England, and this was long before the internet.

We wrote letters to people if we wanted to talk to someone, and it took forever to get there, and forever to get back to us.

My dad has three sisters and my mum has one sister, and I met my mums family when I was about sixteen, my grandmother, my mums sister, her husband and two children, a boy and a girl who were younger than my brother and I, and it was the first time in my life that I actually got to feel what it was like to have family.

They had arrived in Australia from England to live with us until they could find a place of their own.

It was my Aunty that I felt the closest to, she cooked real home cooked meals and desserts including rhubarb pies which I loved, and I felt that she actually listened to me and really heard what I said, which was very rare in our house, as our parents were busy most of the time with work, or household chores as well as their hobbies, I didn't feel left out really, just lonely sometimes.

I always felt different growing up, everyone in my family had brown hair and brown eyes where as I had blonde hair and green eyes so we would always joke I was the milk mans, I wasn't because I have seen my birth certificate but I always wondered before I had seen it.

It was so rare to have someone in my family who wasn't my parents or my brother, I had never experienced that before, to have other people who knew my parents since they were kids was really bizarre for me, especially only growing up with the four of us.

In all the time I knew them, I never really knew them, the kids were too young for me to really get to know them, my grandmother was from the older generation, and my uncle was pretty cool at the time, I remembered him smoking pipes and letting us kids sit on his lap at times, but that's about it.

I remember thinking we weren't a normal family after watching many other families together but they were mine, and to be honest I didn't really know any different.

Life carried on when they moved into their own home, we all went back to doing the things we did before they came into our lives.

We didn't see them again until I gave birth to my second daughter, she was just a newborn when we got the call that my uncle had passed away.

That was really shocking for us as he had passed away at such a young age, and after the funeral it was once again back to normal, no contact, which is strange but true, not sure why, but I guess life just happens.

I kind of just got used to having no other family around, but had a few close friends that shared their wonderful families with me. When I was about sixteen my fathers youngest sister came to visit from England with her young son, he was such a cutie, and he was such a sweet little thing.

I loved having them both in the house, it was so nice having a toddler in the house, and it was so amazing having my aunt in the house, she was closer to my age by only ten years, so we got along great, we had so much fun together and we had a ball while she was there.

My aunt was the first person in the family to keep in contact with me and made the effort to stay in contact after the internet and facebook made it easier to connect years later.

When she left to go back home, I missed her so much, and my little cousin too, I knew I would miss his cute little face forever.

About sixteen years or so later, my cute little cousin passed away suddenly, his life had taken a few bumps and turns as most of our lives do, but the next thing he knew, he had died and was now in spirit, I was shocked to see his spirit years and years later, but was heart warmed at the same time, I had questions like what had taken so long, and where had he been all this time.

He later told me that his death was an exit point for him which he was unaware of at the time, but once he had crossed over he understood for the first time.

An exit point is a few places in our lives where we choose to leave this world, we can leave at anytime during those exit points or we can choose to stay, so if you choose to leave at that point, you will.

There is a religious based stigma around suicide that you go to hell, or you become a lost soul in limbo, but please these are just not true, these are all written by men who put them into a book just so that they could control the masses, this is not what Source / God wanted or said!

These are man made words and since no one except the ones that have crossed over know for sure then I'm going to trust them first.

These are not evil spirits, they are not going to send me to hell, these are just kind, loving, beautiful souls that were once human beings just like us, and I am yet to come across one that is doomed to hell or likes to torment me in a horrible way, and do you know why?.

I will not allow anything negative in my life, the only thing to fear is fear itself, if you believe that you have an evil spirit that will haunt and scare you, it will, if you believe that you will go to hell for believing in a God you don't believe in, then you will, you create your own reality and I have proven that to myself by changing the way I think.

As soon as I refused to live in fear nothing scared me, as soon as I said, "Nothing and no one can hurt me, I will not allow it."Nothing ever has, in fact I fear nothing anymore.

So please, " Think first and feel second", like my friend Erik likes to say.

Now I would like to tell you about an experience I had last week, I had just found a picture of my aunt and my cousin from when they had visited when I was young, and I heard my cousin ask me if I would send it to my aunt, so I told him, " Sure, I will do it in the morning",and then he said, " She could really use it right now if that's ok?", so I sent it.

He then proceeded to ask me if I would tell her that he loved her and that he was sorry.

So off I went to bed thinking she may be comforted by this, and that my cousin would be really happy that I had sent the message, and he would leave me be for a while, not that I didn't like having him because I do, but its nice to have a break from spirit sometimes, but was I wrong, all night I had Peter Allan who had been with me all week for some reason and my cousin singing the song Tentafield Saddler all night long, and I mean all night long, and in the morning I asked my husband what the heck Tentafield Saddler meant other than the song, and he said, "I have no clue, why don't you google it?", so I did.

I found the lyrics to the song and sent them to my aunt who had no idea about the song other than she had heard of it but that's it, so my cousin told me to tell her it's about the words, so I asked her to really read the words, as they are the message, and would you believe she actually knew exactly what he was talking about, apparently the song was pretty much my cousins life, and some of the words talked about things that only my aunt and my cousin knew about, so it was proof for her that her son was talking to me, as I feel the messages I sent previously although appreciated, weren't real proof that he was around her, but this song did, so this was his Christmas gift for her, absolute proof that he was there with her not only during normal times but especially through the holidays.

Such a beautiful gesture, and when the message was received loud and clear, my cousin and Peter Allen blew me and my aunt a kiss and they left, leaving me feeling loved but free since the night before, as much as I love helping the living connect with their loved ones, it can also be draining too, and some people have no clue as to how much energy it takes to do a reading, but this is my life now and I love it.

I have learnt so much from spirit, they are loving, non judgemental, and honest and that is so refreshing when you are surrounded by many people who are the opposite in this world.

Being an Empath, I can always tell when someone is not telling me the truth, I have always had that ability, even as a kid.

It feels very disrespectful to me, why lie when you could just tell the truth? People always find out in the end anyway so what is the point?

I am guilty of this too, I used to lie so people would not get hurt, because I thought that if I lied and they didn't get hurt then I was doing a good thing for them, but let me tell you, it doesn't work that way, people always find out, one way or another and its better to hear the truth from you than from hearing it from someone else after you have lied.

So please think before you speak, there are many Empaths in this world who have this ability, and they may straight up ask you if you are lying, and that wont be a very comfortable conversation.

I rarely call people out on their lies, only because I try to pick my battles these days, and sometimes its just not worth the hassle for me anyway, but think about that next time you think you may lie to someone as they may just call you out, as I do sometimes if I think its necessary.

When I was eighteen, my dad's side of the family came to visit, we had my fathers mother, his sister and my cousin who was about seven at the time, I believe, she was a sick little girl, she was in a wheel chair, she couldn't communicate, and I know she had a huge amount of other things wrong with her but I was just a kid myself and I had had no experience with children really, and especially no experience with a child with disabilities at all, and I had no clue if she could really understand anything that was said.

Us kids were not told much, just that she was sick, and it broke my heart that I could talk, walk, run etc when she couldn't, she would look at me, it felt like she was looking right into my soul and I felt as though she wanted to be just like me, and it made mevery sad.

I could feel her words in my head, I could hear what she was saying but it was like her words had been put directly in my head, so I thought I was just being crazy again and must be making it up, I didn't know at the time that I was talking to her telepathically.

Children who are special often have a direct line to Source / God, they are born with other ways of using their senses, they are very special children, have a look in their eyes, they see and hear more than you could ever realise.

She would tell me it was so hard in that body, because she wanted to do the things I could do, and that she wanted to play with me too, but her body wouldn't let her.

I felt at the time that she wouldn't get very old, I felt her life was literally slipping away, and I was right, a few months after her return to England she passed away.

I was told on my eighteen[th] birthday, I got a call from my mother at my birthday get together, she told me she had passed away, and immediately I saw her being born to me, as my child, and once I realised what I had just seen in the vision I dismissed it, I figured again I was just nuts, I had no real way of knowing that, and I figured I would never really know if she did, but when I gave birth to my first daughter I knew without a doubt that my cousin had come back to me as my daughter this time, and with that she would get a perfect body, a perfect life (for her), she had chosen to reincarnate and that was such a beautiful moment for me.

I didn't really know much about anything with my aunt, uncle and cousin, because they spent most of their time looking after my cousin, and children don't really understand the sacrifices that people make for their children, it doesn't really give them time for anything else in life, but they do it out of love

I would be so jealous of the fact that other people got to experience grandparents that loved them and cooked for them, and hugged them, I just didn't have that at all.

That was all I had ever wanted growing up, but isn't that what we all look for growing up?, we all want what we don't have, and the ones that do, don't always appreciate what they have.

My life was a series of events that have been up and down, I had good days and bad days as most of us do, but because of what I experienced, I didn't write about my story so I could get sympathy, or for people to be judgemental, I wrote about it because unless you know about my past, you wont really understand my future, as its all connected.

There are many people in this world who will try to make you feel bad about yourself, or make you feel like that you have to do what society expects of you, or will try and map out the future they want you to have, not what you want for yourself, and you might feel as though you have no other choice but to do what is expected of you, and if that is what you want to do then go ahead and do it if it makes you happy.

I want you to really look inside yourself and see what it is that makes you happy, or If your at that stage where you are not sure what makes you happy then take the time you need to get to that point, take a trip, work a mundane job, take a year off, whatever you want to do to find your way, there is no hurry, no matter what anyone says, you will find what makes you happy in your own time, I didn't find what makes me happy until I was well into my 40's so don't worry if it doesn't come straight away.

What it came down to is this, you can't control how other people feel about you, not even the two people in the whole world who are meant to love you unconditionally.

It says more about the kind of people they are than it does about you, and sometimes you just have to accept that they mean well but they are not you, and they don't know what your path is meant to look like and they also don't know what is in your heart, some people may try to control you, and some people just want what is best for you, either way work out what you want and then go for it, if other people can't handle it, well that is their problem not yours, you have your own life to live and you shouldn't let other people get in your way, but always be respectful when disagreeing with someone, say thankyou for caring, but I have my own life to live and no one can live it but me, you can either be on board with that or not, but I would prefer to have you in my life, but that is your choice.

For your own mental health you need to do what makes you happy.

It's not worth the heartache to sit and let it fester, just release it and move on, because only you can make yourself happy, you can't rely on others to do it for you.

The best part of my life was when I decided not to let people dim my light, to not let people control me, once I decided that my life was mine to control and not for others to, I finally found the courage to become what I have always wanted to become, because I no longer had fear.

I became a medium, which I would never have had the nerve to become while toxic people were still in my life, so I have taken a negative experience and I have turned it into a positive one.

Becoming a medium has given me a sense of purpose, a sense of belonging in a world where people love me for who I am, and don't judge me for being me.

My own husband and children have been fantastic supports for me, and although some of them don't really believe in what I believe, they accept it as being a part of me, and that's all I could ask for as a wife and mother, it makes me so happy to be surrounded by a family that believes in me, even if they don't exactly believe I spirits or don't want to believe.

Makes me so proud of the children I have raised, that they can put their feelings aside to help support me, because they know how much it means to me.

Around seven years ago an event happened in my life that changed me, it turned my life upside down and made me rethink everything and everyone in my life, it tore me apart and to be honest it has taken a lot of courage and healing to forgive and forget.

When something like this happens to you where you start to wonder if anyone in your life can be trusted then you need to start again, start from the ground up, look at everything in your life and re evaluate what is important and what isn't, look after yourself, do things that make you happy, simple things like read a book, watch a marathon of your favourite movies, have a spa day, ride your motorbike etc whatever makes you happy and then think about how you want to proceed with your life, are the people in it making your life hell? Get rid of them then.

You don't owe anyone anything, if they cant accept you for who you are then they need or they need to go, don't let anyone dim your light, your here for a reason, you have a job to do, what that job is only your soul knows, so that is why its so important for you to do what makes you happy.

You should know though that we do pick the people in our life before we incarnate, we pick them for what they can do for us in life, and what we can do for them, sometimes we think why?

Why would we pick those people as our parents or siblings or friends when they are so cruel to us?, and other times we are happy with who we pick, either way, like it or not, they are our the people we have chosen to learn from and whom we teach, these people help us one way or another, whether its to learn trust, love, confidence, protectiveness, friendship whatever.

When you get older you start to realise what it is that we learnt from them, but think of it this way, they loved us enough to agree to incarnate with us to help us do what we needed to do to live out our lives and to grow our souls, for example no one who didn't love you that much would choose to be a cruel parent, or a lousy parent, or even a great parent, but remember this, if you had really good parents who did everything for you to the point that your a spoilt brat who thinks everyone should do everything for you, what do you think you would learn from that?

What if your souls purpose here on earth was to learn compassion and love? Do you think you could learn those things in that situation? No, so then something would have to happen to help you learn those things, so maybe your very nice parents suddenly die in a car accident and leave you broke and alone, with no friends to support you because they only liked you for your money and now that its gone they don't want anything to do with you, and suddenly life is nothing like it started out like.

Sometimes things have to change to help us get to where we need to go, and sometimes that change can hurt us, or even break us, especially when it's done by someone who is meant to love you.

For me to become a medium I needed to lose the people that would never have allowed me to become one, there is a good chance they had a completely different reason for leaving than we think, they feel the need to do it for their own path and needs, and we go on and live our lives to the best of our abilities.

I have seen people who lived in a perfect bubble of their lives, who would say their life is perfect, then they suddenly lose their child to a disease, murder or an accident etc and then they say, "Why us?", we lived good lives, we went to church every week, we loved each other well, and then suddenly they decide they don't want this to happen to any other parent, they want to let people know about the risks and that it can happen to anyone no matter how good or bad your life is.

They decide to start a charity in their loved ones name and then they start talking in schools to other children to talk about the dangers of....etc etc and the they save hundreds of other children from suffering the same fate as their child.

This was the life plan of the original child, for those children to be saved that child needed to die, it sounds terrible and a waste of life I know, but often they come into this life knowing how and when they will die and knowing the changes they will make by dying that way and the lives they will save by living out that life.

This is a life plan, and this is how it's like a domino effect, these special people choose to come into this life to make a difference and they do, in a big way they do.

So it's hard to blame anyone for the decisions they make or things that are done to them, or even accidents that happen to them, even though you really feel you want or need to blame someone, this is all part of their life plan, and you have one too, but most are just not aware of what that will be and that is ok, it doesn't really matter, the point is to just live you life the way if feels it needs to be led, and do the best you can with what you have, all will become clear in time.

To lose ones parents or children can feel like a massive hole in your heart, but to lose parents or children because they don't want to be around you, can lead you down a spiralling road where it feels like there is no return Think though how this can make your life better and not how it can make it worse, it gives you a chance to do things for yourself and not for others, it gives you a chance to shine.

I could have and almost did fall in a heap of no return, when I lost important people in my life, I just couldn't understand how someone who was supposed to love me could just walk away like I never existed.

I won't lie, it hurt but I turned it around and made it an advantage for me, I always wanted to pursue mediumship but was too scared the people in my life would disown me, they did anyway so I was able to pursue at my own leisure with out the fear of the backlash from them.

But that didn't stop the fear of others walking away from me, but I shouldn't have worried, I was meant to do something I loved and being a medium is what I love.

So do what you are born to do, don't let anyone or anything get in your way, if you have a burning desire to be a medium but your a lawyer which you don't like doing, take the plunge, don't worry what people will think, it doesn't matter because they aren't the ones that have to live your life or walk in your shoes.

I could have been a medium years ago, I have had the ability since I was a child, but I was scared what people would say, and they had already basically told me it was all nonsense anyway, so I believed they would walk away from me if they found out.

Well they walked away anyway but for a completely different reason, so don't wait to do what you love for fear of reprisal, just do it anyway, people may not support you anyway, or you might be surprised like I was and have people who love and support you anyway, no matter what you choose to do.

They are the people you want in your life, people who know what you do and don't care, as long as your happy, they are happy, they are your real friends and real family, and sometimes you have to create your own family if your own refuse to support you, and good friends, spouses, children etc will be there for you no matter what if they love you, so don't worry if there are people who don't support you, you just need to realise that if they are meant to be around you forever they will, and if they aren't then they won't and there is nothing we can do about that, it's out of our control.

My Favourite Quote -

"What people think of me, is none of my business". - Eleanor Roosevelt

CHAPTER 2

Bullying and inappropriate behavior

When I was around thirteen, I had met a girl that lived on the same street as the bus stop that I caught the bus at when I was going to my high school, she told me about an old man that lived a few houses down from that bus stop that she visited form time to time to cook or bake for him and in return he gave her cigarettes so she asked me to go with her so I did, I didn't see the harm in it, since he was old and was like a great grandfather figure, so we went over there and she introduced him to me and I thought he seemed nice but kind of creepy, but she said he was really cool and that I shouldn't judge him, he gave her smokes, so how bad could he be, and he had said he had kids and grand kids so I didn't really I should judge, but I was starting to realise that she didn't know him as well as she thought, and that confused me because she made it sound like she had known him for years, but I was coming to the conclusion that she was lying to me.

So we visited this man and we baked him cakes, or helped tidy up the house, and he would give us cigarettes in return, over the next few months we continued to visit him, but each time I felt there was something about him that was making my stomach turn.

My warning system would get stronger and stronger each time we went there, but my friend kept insisting that he was fine, nice even.

One day we went over there and he said, "Come and look in my room", my warning bells went off like crazy but my friend said, " Yeah come take a look", so we did.

He said, " I want to show you something, but in order to show you, you need to take your pants off", he told us we had to put the quilt over our head, I didn't want to but he said I had to, but I all I wanted to do was run and never look back.

My friend said, " Come on I promise its funny", not having any clue as to what he was planning to do, I went along with it, although I was starting to totally freak out by this stage, and then he did the unthinkable, he touched me between my legs, it was just for a split second before I jumped up and pulled up my pants so fast I nearly fell over, he said, " It's ok just lay back down and don't move, I wont hurt you", and my friend said, " It's ok he has done it to me before and its ok, its good".

I told her that we shouldn't be here and that we needed to go home now!

She said, " you can go, I'm fine, you are gutless?", I did not have a good feeling about I said no, I said you need to come with me now, but she just started yelling at me to go, and I knew that if I stayed, something bad was going to happen, so I left.

I was pure, and I had never ever even thought about it, in fact it wasn't something that I knew anything about, all I knew was that I was not getting a good feeling about it, and I knew what he was doing was wrong, he was a man old enough to be my great grandfather.

As I left to walk home by myself, I was shaking and crying, I was so scared for my friend, I was actually terrified for her.

The whole night I was so worried about if she was home yet, and what he had done to her, I literally cried all night.

The next day, she was on the bus when I got on and I asked her what had happened when I had left and she said, " I don't know what you are talking about ", I tried to say about the old man but she told me to shut up and that we were not friends any more!.

I was so confused, I didn't know if I had done something wrong, she didn't talk to me at all after that and when I got off the bus after school that day, there were grown men and a few girls my age including my friends and the friend from the bus, they were standing out the front of a house near the bus stop, and they were waiting to beat her up and they were waiting until I walked past them to hurt me, the girl had told them that I had tried to beat her up, and they were hoping to do the same to me, I said, " I didn't do anything to her", but then she called me a liar.

I started crying because these men started saying horrible things to me, and they said they were going to get me from my bed one night and then I will wish I had let them hurt me that day.

I ran all the way home in tears, and I told my dad what was happening, and he made me get into the car with him, and we drove there together.

Everyone was still there and they were laughing and drinkingalcohol, and my dad got out of the car while I was still in there and he was yelling at them that they need to pick on someone their own size, and that they could try hitting him if they want, but nothing happened in the end and we left, and on the car ride home my dad kept saying, "what did you do, what did you do?", I told him I had no idea why they were after me, I had no idea what I had done to deserve it.

My father didn't believe me, he thought I had done something bad and he grounded me, he said I had put him in a bad situation.

I have never been so confused in my life, I had absolutely no clue as to why this had happened to me.

It wasn't until years later that it had occurred to me the circumstances as to which I had left her in that day, she could have been raped by the old man, I hadn't realised that would happen at the time, I didn't even know what that word was, nor even what sex was, and for a while there, for maybe a few years, I blamed myself for leaving her there, even though she made me go, but in the mind of a child I couldn't understand.

I really wished I had of made her go that day but I couldn't, I was just a child too and I didn't understand, and neither did she, we had grown up quite isolated to that part of life, I didn't know it could happen, but the old man did, and what he did to us that day has haunted me for years, its something ill never forget though, but its something I had to forgive him for, although I doubt I will ever forget.

I know that the old man died years ago, but I hope that girl reported it because I never did, I always thought it was my fault and if I hadn't put myself in that position then it wouldn't have happened.

I know now that I'm an adult that it was not my fault, I didn't know what could happen, the old man did and it was his fault, and no one else's.

I hope that girl got help for what happened if what I think happened, and she has managed to live a relatively normal life.

I have never heard from her again, as her family moved away around six months after it happened from memory, but I never spoke to her again either after that day.

Although I did see her for about six months after that incident, she just wasn't ever the same person again though, the same innocent little girl that she was, something changed in her that day and now I think I know why, I just wished I could have spoken to her about it, and to let her know that it wasn't her fault, because no matter what he had done to her before, I just don't think it was anything like what he did to her that day, I now know he was grooming her.

I know she blamed herself for not going when I told her she should go, and I know she blamed me because I wasn't there to protect her.

What we both didn't realise at the time was that we could have spoken up, we could have told an adult, I know our parents probably wouldn't have believed us but I should have told someone, and I wish I had, looking back I wish I had called the police and had him charged or at least told an adult who could have done it for me.

Just so you know, its not ok for someone to do that to you, and it's not ok for an adult to take advantage of a child, no matter what they say, or what they do, the minute you can get away, you need to let an adult you trust know so they can report it for you, or you need to call the police yourself, but either way, do not believe for one second that you deserve any of it, you don't, so if anything like this is happening or worse has or is happening to you please, please tell someone now, right now, go on, do it right now!!! Remember that you are more than likely not the only person this has happened to or is happening to, and not everyone knows that it is illegal and wrong for someone to do that to you but it is, and I guarantee that if you don't report it, they will do it to someone else, you see he was hoping to groom me too, but I was lucky that I knew it was wrong and went with my instincts.

So if you won't do it for yourself, do it for the next child that it may happen to, because once they do it once, they almost always do it again.

Also please talk to a councillor at your your school, or there are hot lines you can call in your area, just use google to find one, or the phone book.

Bullying, physical abuse and metal abuse runs rampant in most schools, homes and in society, and many children have to deal with it day in and day out from parents / family members, other children, teachers and other adults in the community.

Most people don't even realise they are bullying someone else, most times they think what they are doing is funny, well deserved, or just do it because their friends are.

Until the bully gets bullied themselves they generally don't realise how it affects the other person being bullied.

I have been bullied so many times in my life starting in day care, then primary school, then high school, and even in adulthood, there has been many a time that I have sat in my room crying thinking I didn't have a friend in the world, both of my parents worked hard long hours so I spent a lot of time in my own thoughts, its a horrible feeling to feel so alone.

By the time I was in my teens, I had not only bullying to deal with, but I also had all the triggers that come from being a teenager, I felt alone and upset, I felt like I wasn't worthy and to top it off, the raging hormones that tend to bowl us over when we get to this precarious time in our lives had just taken hold, it was one of the worst times in my life, I spent so long just rebelling against everything and everyone, and I felt I had been given a raw deal.

Looking back I can look at that time objectively now, but at the time I couldn't, I feel very lucky I survived it to be honest.

What people need to think about at this time, is that your not alone, no matter how you feel there is always someone you can talk to, whether its a teacher, a parent of a friend, your parent, a friend, or just someone you trust.

Also make sure that you yourself talk to people like you would like to be spoken to, its not difficult to be nice to people, even if they are not nice to you, Its not ok to make someone feel bad because you do or because your friends are, or even just to be hurtful.

Are you being bullied?, or are you a bully?, that is something I want people to really think about.

I have been a bully a few times in my life, once as a bully who hurt someone for no reason, and I got in a few fights standing up for myself, and sometimes standing up for my brother when he was little.

The one that remains in my mind to this very day was when I was very young, I was in primary school, my parents had some new friends over at the house who were German and hadn't been in Australia very long, they had two children, a boy and a girl who were both around the same age as my brother and I.

I don't remember their sons name but I will always remember their daughter's name for as long as I live, her name was Karin, and I live everyday with the knowledge of what I did to her.

She had come into my brothers room with me which I believe my brother and I were sharing at the time, we had bunk beds and we had come in to play so we shut the door.

I asked her what her name was and she said Karin, I said, "What, Karin, I think your name is wrong, I think its supposed to be Karen",but she said no its Karin, and I again said the same thing, and then I wouldn't let her leave the room until she said her name was Karen, she started crying so I let her out, and she went to her parents saying I was being mean, which I denied.

Karin, her brother and their parents left straight after that, and my parents questioned me about being mean to her, but again I denied it, I personally don't think they believed me but they dropped it.

I felt so guilty for so long, wondering why I had to be so mean.

Then when I was eighteen I was at my boss's house for Christmas drinks with his wife, friends and other staff.

I turned around and saw her sitting with some other kids, so I went up and said hi and asked if I could speak to her, she said yes, so we went somewhere a bit quieter and I told her that I had wanted to apologise for what I had done to her all those years before, and do you know what she said?, well she said, " I have no idea what your talking about Alana, I don't remember you ever being mean to me".

Well she could have bowled me over with a stick I was so surprised, but I was glad she didn't remember, or she just didn't want to remember, I guess I will never really know, but I do know that I deserved to remember it, because it reminded me that bullying is not ok, and remembering her tears is enough to remind me of that.

You may say, well that wasn't bad, but it was to me, I upset a girl for no other reason other than I was being bullied and I saw her as being vulnerable and decided to be a bully myself, and that is not ok.

I got into a fight when I was about sixteen years old, a girl who I didn't know, who I had only met a few times, but hadn't really spoken to had told my friends some lies about me, and I had no clue as to why she would do that, they were really nasty things she said and it really upset me, and a few friends of mine started saying, " are you going to let her get away with that?", and started revving me up to go and talk to her about it, so we did.

I went up to her and asked her why she was talking lies about me, and she mumbled something back that was horrendous so I hit her, just once, but it was enough, it was a stupid mistake, I let my anger get the better of me, but I couldn't take it back even if I wanted to.

I then went home and felt really stupid that I couldn't control my emotions, why couldn't I have just left her alone and not gone near her in the first place?

Well to be honest I was too emotionally insecure and unequipped to handle a response like that when I was so immature.

So the next thing I knew the police came around, and she was charging me with assault.

Excellent, so off I went to court two years later, that is how long it took to go through, and by that stage I was nineteen and around six months pregnant, so I felt very stupid and really embarrassed, and not only that I was a different person by then.

I got community service because they agreed that what she had done was uncalled for, however my actions were also uncalled for, so off I went and spent my work day hours at a short term housing place where people who were needing housing for a short time until they found something else would go like, domestic violence sufferers or people who had been kicked out of their previous houses etc.

It was the best thing that had ever happened to me, I loved it, and it helped me to get a good job later on, and I got some great skills working there too, I also met some amazing women and I just really enjoyed working there until it closed down not long after.

I never did anything stupid like that again, it really scared me going into court by myself with no support while being pregnant.

I'm glad I learnt from those times, I needed to know it was not ok to hurt people, I should have known better, I had been bullied my whole life and then I went and did it to someone else, and that is not ok.

All life is precious and how we talk to people and treat people makes a difference, you just don't know what someone is already going through before you start your bullying, your words can and do hurt, so think before you speak, always try to be kind and don't do things because your friends think it's funny.

I want you to look at the person your bullying and I want you to imagine that it's you that it's happening to, is it funny yet?, do you feel proud now at the way your behaving?

You can change this, if you are a bully already it's not too late to change your way of thinking, and your actions, stand up and be the human being you were meant to be, be kind, compassionate, loving, and you can make a difference, you can stop what your doing and tell your friends your not ok with this, that you won't be hurting these people anymore.

You have the power to stand in your own power, so do it, do it for yourself, do it for your family, or do it for whoever you feel the need to do it for, but most of all do it for the person you are bullying.

Be the change you want to see in others!

I asked my friends to tell me their bullying stories, whether they were the bully or were bullied, and I must say I was really surprised at how many stepped forward and told me their stories, every single person I asked had been bullied as a child or even as an adult, every single one, and I spoke to over 30 people, and not one said, "Oh I was never bullied".

That really surprised me, I knew that many people each day went through bullying but I really had no idea how many there really were, and remember I only spoke to thirty people and each and every one of them were bullied, so think about that.

I'm betting that as you are reading this, your thinking about when you were bullied, how many times you were bullied, and for how long, so please just know you are not alone like I mentioned before, and as you will see everyone has their own story, and it breaks my heart that so many people can be so cruel to each other, but what makes these stories special is that each and every person I spoke to managed to turn their hurt around and turn it into a positive, these people are really my hero's, it takes a lot of guts to take something that could literally destroy you and turn it into a positive by then helping others in a similar situation, or by finding themselves and doing what they love, they are not letting the bully win, and that takes a huge amount of determination.

The love these people have for themselves is truly inspiring, they love who they are and they will no longer allow people to get inside their heads and that takes so much courage.

While I was reading about my friends experiences I was in tears, to think of these beautiful, loving human beings I call my friends, and being bullied like they were made me realise what a huge problem bullying was and still is in this world, will it ever end?

I think it needs to start right here, right now and if your reading this, you were meant to, and I want you to think about your life andwhat you can do to change how you treat people yourself, taking that one step to make sure the people around you are safe and loved, and to make sure that kid at school or person at work has a voice if they can't do it themselves, because you have no idea what they deal with at home, at school etc you just see what you see at that moment, and if it's a terrible thing to watch, then imagine how terrible it would be to endure.

Stand up and make yourself proud!

I have watched my eight year old daughter get bullied from her first day at school, and the teachers have done nothing, they don't see the tears I see when she comes home, they don't see the hurt in her eyes that people could be so mean to her, when all she wants in this world is for everyone to love each other and to be kind to each other.

They say bullying in schools is not tolerated, well I can tell you from experience that most teachers turn a blind eye to it, and generally they punish the child who is getting bullied for dobbing, and that is NOT on!

Who is going to be the voice for these people?, and who is going to be the voice for our children if their own teachers, friends or parents cant or wont.

When you look in your child's eyes and see them hurt and in pain because of bullying and you have to explain to them why this is happening to them what all they want to do is be friends with everyone then maybe you may understand how much bullying affects everyone.

I'm not saying all teachers turn a blind eye but I have seen many, for many years do it, there are some who are kind and caring to children getting bullied, but to the ones that let it happen, you should be ashamed of yourself, would you do the same if it was your child getting bullied?, I don't believe you would.

So a word of advice to the adults that teach and watch our children during the school hours when we are not there to protect our children, listen to the children that come to tell you they are being hurt, bullied and harassed and actually take action, because if you don't, these kids who are in your care can either become much worse bullies or if they are being bullied can eventually hurt or kill themselves and this is on you, you will have to live with that because you were too busy or stressed out in your own life to care.

We teach our children that the teachers are there to help, and when you don't help, when you let our children down, our children may not tell anyone else, they will just keep quiet and endure it, because if their own teachers wont stop the horror, who will?

Well it's time we all stood up and said, "That is not ok."

Do it for your brother, your sister, your parents, whoever you need to do it for, even for yourself, and like I said before, "Be the change you want to see in others."

This is from a friend of mine who has come so far in her spiritual journey in such a short time, these are her memories of her experiences that everyone can learn from, and not unlike my own story, she is someone who took her experiences and turned them into a positive, and I'm so very proud of the woman she has become, I hope you enjoy her story as much as I did.

I guess you could say I was born awake or at the very least close to it, I was sensitive and curious about everything as a child, that attribute didn't make me very popular amongst my Sunday school teacher and pastors in the church that I went to.

I had a lonely childhood growing up because I just simply didn't fit in and most of my peers thought I was weird or strange and for reasons I never understood didn't like me.

Before I went to school I was always hamming it up for relatives and going out of my way to make them laugh, until around grade two when I stopped and went into my shell and started daydreaming of adventures.

I used to imagine some mythical creature smashing the window of the school and rescuing me.

I never liked school and pulled up every tactic I could conjure up not to go, I had a hard time understanding what was being taught and didn't see the point in learning things like history or math.

I never felt smart and my grades only reflected that back to me, I was always creative however and enjoyed writing and poetry but was too shy to read them out loud.

I was aware of children whispering about me, caught every dirty look thrown at me, even when I was way across the other side of the room.

I didn't know how I knew, I could just feel it, I could also read what the kids were thinking and it was so uncomfortable and caused me to become very shy and subconscious.

When I was around seven years old, I would spend my Saturdays completely absorbed in this book my mom had, called "Into the Unknown" it was all about Telekinesis, ESP, Psychic Abilities, UFO's and Hauntings, I read that book cover to cover looking at all the pages and articles and was fascinated and drawn to it.

Something stirred in me that I couldn't explain, it was my favourite book and I wanted to learn more, of course it was completely against the religion that the paranormal. I asked questions about UFO's and Dinosaurs with my teachers and didn't get answers that satisfied me.

When I was twelve, I started hanging around this new friend all the time who was a Mormon and I wanted to be one too, my parents allowed us to choose our beliefs so they agreed to allow me to be baptised, it wasn't very long after that, that I decided that it wasn't for me, while it was against the rules to eat chocolate because it had caffeine in it, although I gave up on religion, I never became an atheist either.

I always believed there was a GOD and I believed in UFO's and ET's too, just no way to tie them all together to make it fit.

It was years later when I was in my twentie's that I finally got my answers and that was after discovering Sylvia Browne, I couldn't get enough of her and bought so many of her books, it was as if she shined a light on everything I had been searching for.

Everything she wrote about resonated so strongly with me, I would like to say she is credited with my remembering more that awakening, but definitely was what brought me where I am today and I will always be grateful to her as well as my guides for guiding me and putting the right people and circumstances in my path.

I can honestly say now that after so many years I know why I feel things energetically and know things, I am an Empath and a Clairsentient Starseed who is still on the journey of remembering as well as developing my own gifts, I am also a healer and lightworker who is here to help raise the consciousness of the planet.

I have had many hardships but also many blessings, my experiences have led me into the profession of life coaching and I wouldn't change a thing, I also came out of my shell and now embrace my inner dork with a spiritual twist.

– Written by Jody Baumel.

CHAPTER 3

How bullying effects everyone

A s I mentioned before, I asked some of my friends if they would like to share their bullying stories with me, and I had figured that now they were adults, they would be able to look back on their experiences and be objective and at the very least have gotten over their experiences, but boy was I wrong, and this included myself as well, as I had thought I too would have been over the hurt but wow talk about triggering memories that I had forgotten all about.

I found out that not only did we go through such a terrible time when we were younger, but most of us had tried to just forget about it until I had asked us all to relive it.

It brought up so much emotion for them, that I realised that bullying is not just something we go through growing up, it's also something we take with us into adulthood, or try to suppress deep down into ourselves.

We never get over that hurt, that feeling of loneliness, and the feelings of abandonment.

We may forgive that it happened but we certainly never forget, and I found that people who hurt me as a teenager wanted to be friends with me later on in life, because most had forgotten how they had treated me, or they had forgotten or didn't recognise me as being the one they hurt.

So I say this to all of you, whether you are the person bullying people or if you are the person being bullied, think about what is happening in your life at home, then think about that you have no clue what someone else Is going through, you have no clue, even if you think you know, you really don't.

So I want you to think about that, you don't know that your words and your fists can do to a person, you don't know if they are already getting that at home or if it's worse at home, there is a good chance it's happening there too, so your actions can tip a person over the edge, they may decide that no one could ever love them, that they are useless, not worthy of friendship etc.

If their family at home could do it to them and the people at school can do it to them, where else do they have to turn?

If that person then decides to take their life and do succeed, then you are just as much to blame for their death as their family is, and that is on you!

So please think about that before you bully someone again, and if you are the victim of bullying, please again know that you are not alone, there Is help available, please go onto Google and look up support centres that deal with bullying, there are many, or talk to your teacher, or family member, just tell someone that you trust, and get some help, but most of all, send your bullies love, sounds strange? Yes I know, but if you send them love, it will get to them and believe it or not it will help, I know, I have done it myself.

Now I want to share with you how this experience has affected other people

This is Jan's story

I was bullied by a girl in my gymnastics team at a very young age, and this pattern has continued throughout my life.

The girl that bullied me in the team I was in, was extremely jealous of me because of my talent.

As I got better and better I got chosen over her constantly, and I know it was very hard on her for me to come in and take her spot that she had held for over five years before I got there, but she was vicious to me, and it was abusive.

I never said anything to her and I kept accelerating in my position which made it worse for her.

The leader of the group gave me most of the attention that was needed to help me excel and the attention was then off her.

She made snide comments all the time and made extremely cruel remarks about my body and my personality.

I was so well behaved and disciplined that she was just part of my challenge to over come just like an injury or something.

I had far worse things happen to me than her.

This type of behaviour and person has been an ongoing theme throughout my life since then.

There has been a female in so many of the groups, jobs, and classes that have been severely jealous of me and they have been abusive too.

I do not know them or had any real conflict with them, they just come out of nowhere and just start.

It is obvious to me that there is a window of opportunity open to them within me for them to come over and do this.

A place for them to vent, I represent a threat usually though for some reason, and they are afraid I am going to take away something of theirs.

It has been a very uncomfortable theme to live through because it happens in every job or place I go.

I do work very hard at everything I do and I do excel, I do not try and step on anyone's toes, and I do not want to take anyone's friends, partner's, jobs, or status or anything away from anyone.

It is amazing to watch this now that I am older, as this theme has not yet stopped.

I guess I still haven't healed this totally yet.

I have been attacked, among many other things that are too personal for me to disclose, but this is something I have always lived with throughout my life.

Written by Jan (aged in her fiftie's)

This is Karin's Story

I have been bullied from kindergarten through all school ears and even through the sixteen years of working, until an accident caused by being bullied at work by my office member and my boss.

They ordered me to climb up to the high placed office windows to clean them which was not part of my job description/contract.

Because of my handicapped legs I stumbled and fell right at the corner of my bosses table and damaged and tore my bladder into countless pieces.

I went to a specialist in urology and they made a check but they couldn't see anything, so they diagnosed me with a kidney infection and they gave me antibiotics and pain pills.

I worked for six months without knowing my bladder was damaged and one morning (it was the first day I had free) I woke up with a temperature of fourty two degree fever and I couldn't stand up because of the immense pain.

That was the moment that I knew I was dying, and I needed to call the professor of urology and get him to meet me at my hospital.

My sister worked near my apartment and she picked me up and took me to emergency, it was a 4 hour drive from my apartment to the hospital and when I got there they stabilised me and then I went through a dangerous surgery, and I almost died during it.

A month later I went back to work at the same job where this accident happened and they wanted me to go and buy things for their private party which was going to happen hours after the office was closed, they were personal items that are not part of the job at all.

I had to carry four, 20kg bags two in each hand, and as I reached the office I had such horrible pain because my wound was over 30cm long and had not yet healed completely.

I told my boss that I wont be able to do that again as my doctor had told me that my limit was 4 pounds, and he got so angry with me that he punched me in the face saying, " You are useless then".

I went to my health insurance and got a letter to say that I can not work anymore, and I don't regret it for an instance.

I am now relatively safe from people like that now that I'm not working anymore.

Written by Karin (in her fiftie's)

This is Sue's story

I was thirteen years old and we had what I think was an Indian guy named Earl at our school, he was a quiet and shy guy which made him likeable to me.

We sometimes talked but generally he kept to himself, I thought his name was really unusual and I noticed that when I coughed, my cough sounded like Earl, Earl.

I went up to him one day and did a fake cough assimilating his name into it, and I laughed but he just stood there starting at me, so I did it again and again until he walked away.

After he went away I thought about his reaction and I realised that instead of thinking I had done something funny, he probably felt embarrassed and it was then that I realised that I was being a bully.

I tracked him down right away and apologised, I felt really ashamed of myself and I told him I would never ever make that joke again.

I didn't realise until later how awful it much have been for him, but he accepted my apology and he was kind to me for the rest of our school days.

I never forgot Earl's powerful response or how stupid I had been,

33

I truly was not seeking power at his expense, I was simply naive and it was thoughtless of me to imagine he would laugh along with me.

It affects me now as a teacher, as I point out to bullies that they made another person feel embarrassed or ashamed and that they have no right to do such a powerful thing.

Written by Sue (aged in her fiftie's)

This is Joanne's story

When I was little, my family was very poor but love was abundant, so I never felt I was lacking in any way.

My mother had to work well before I went to school and I had to get myself ready from year three onwards, and I often went to school without lunch or supplies.

I had a teacher who made us produce handkerchiefs at morning assembly, and everyone had to wave their embroidered white hanky in the air, but because I had no such hanky she stood me up in front of the whole school and had everyone sing about what a little piggy I am.

This happened day after day after day until it was a regular occurrence that kids would pass me and start singing the piggy song.

I spent the majority of my life feeling ugly, inferior and very second class, but I have only noticed recently this root of my own lack of abundance throughout life, feeling undeserving and inferior.

How bullying has affected me

I have always thought of myself (unconsciously it would seem) as second class.

My experience taught me very young that other's have the power to degrade me based upon y financial status, but mostly it taught me to question the value of my self worth.

My mother worked two jobs and I always knew how much she loved me, but I felt if she knew how I was being treated it would break her heart because she could not provide the extras other kids had, so I hid my hurt and shame that I felt about myself from her.

I have been married three times, all to men who I have sought safety and protection from, and all of them objectified me, they told me how to act, how to dress and how to behave, and ultimately discarded me when something better came along, or I stood up for myself and the requirements they expected of me, which then put me back on the poverty line.

Men who have prioritised appearances to boost their own self worth and ego are the ones I always the ones I unconsciously chose and I repeated the hurt, shame and feeling of not being good enough again and again.

How I am continuing to help myself

I am now working to achieve self love, I am finally standing on my own two feet, and I'm raising my two children independently.

I know I have amazing gifts and qualities but I still struggle so much, I constantly struggle to measure up to my peers no matter how I have succeeded in life.

I have three degrees and I am just finishing a masters degree with honours.

I still feel shame because I know my kids do not have all the things they need even though I know they are so proud of me.

I'm just learning the power of my own strength, that I don't need to conform to the wishes of others at all, and that being me is enough if I say its enough, its my choice not anyone else's on how I should be me.

What would I say to bullies now?

Children are so undervalued by the adults that hold their position of power, so I would say look into your heart, does it feel good to humiliate children?

What is so lacking in your heart to feel as though you need to do this?

Look inside to where your inner child is broken and start to feel and stop projecting your inner harm onto others who are innocent.

Message to my child self

You are amazing, you are strong, brave and you have the strength to move mountains, so don't rely on others to provide you with approval.

They do not approve of themselves. I love you and you are love!

Run, jump and feel the joy of the love that surrounds you little one, and don't let attachments and other people's opinion of you slow you down.

Written by Joanne (aged in her fourtie's)

This is Monique's story

I was bullied every single day of school up until grade twelve when I dropped out half way through.

Physical appearance (I have a large nose) and religion (Jehovah witness) means no standing up for the national anthem when you are at school or anywhere else, so I was singled out from day one.

I wasn't allowed to hang out with any kids who were not of the same religion, so again I was singled out.

I was an easy target for kids, I was bullied through stares, snide remarks and I always got picked last for sports and no one wanted to be my partner in activities ad no one wanted to play in the playground with me.

It was a daily struggle just to go to school, walking into a classroom always made me anxious etc.

This played out well into high school where the cafeteria played a roll.

Thank goodness for no internet or cell phones back then.

It affected me by not being talkative, I had trouble expressing myself, and I attempted suicide.

I once sat in my room with a knife, I was running it over my wrists but I couldn't bring myself to do it.

I wrote a suicide note and everything but it always made me worry what people would think of me, being that my religion says that suicides go to hell.

I worried how I looked and how I acted, so eventually I looked for love in all the wrong places, resorting to sexually orientated conversation's and humour to connect and get people to like me.

I lied to make myself appear better, at least I thought I appeared better, I ran away from home because I couldn't stand the religious restrictions any more.

I got pregnant in year twelve and I dropped out of high school, I left because a class I had which was a law class was all about standing up in front of people, and the bullies in my life were all in that class too, so I dropped out in fear of what was expected in class and who was in it.

The results of fifteen years of bullying was that I had zero self confidence, I used sexual innuendo's as a way for people to like me, I was always worried what other people saw in me, and this has stayed with me for thirty three years.

Once someone at school held a pencil upright on my chair as I sat down and it pierced my bottom so bad it was bleeding and I was only in grade four or five, I was so embarrassed and very very sore.

In grade one I had an accident in my snow pants and someone went running and told everyone.

Kids wrote nasty things on my locker, years later and the list goes on and on.

I don't feel the pain of it any more as it has helped me by talking about it and sharing it with others.

The pain used to follow me to work, it followed me in to new friendships and I am happy to report that the severity of what I felt is almost gone, because I'm learning to self love and to not worry so much about what people think.

Monique also wrote a story to her teenage self that I think that all teenagers need to read:

Dear little lost girl,

I wish I could tell you that everything is going to be ok, and that all of your troubles are far behind you and that you won't cry any more tears.

I wish I could tell you that today is the last day you need to hide your true self..

I wish I could show you the right clothes to wear and how to talk with others so they will like you, I wish, I wish, I wish, don't these words sound familiar?, you use them all the time to hide your pain.

I am happy to tell you though that all the hard times you are going through and will experience will make you this extraordinary, empowering and inspirational woman.

You are married and you have an incredible son.

There are so many tips I have for you, but the main points I want to Learn to love yourself as soon as possible, try not to let the past control your future, and try not to let the future scare you, I want you to have positive thoughts and I want you to be grateful for the life you have.

Your thoughts are powerful, so choose wisely what you are putting your energy into.

As you know growing up as a Jehovah witness puts a lot of pressure on you to be a certain way, talk a certain way and make you hide your true thoughts and feelings out of fear.

Not only do you survive this, it will become one of the building blocks for you to become the person you will become.

Cherish the time you have in the religion and with your family and friends.

The bullies that you have and will continue to face will become another building block to the strong woman you will become.

In your darkest moments just try to imagine why they need to make themselves feel better by hurting you.

What is happening in their own lives that makes them want to belittle someone else to feel good about themselves.

Try not to let them bother you, I know this is hard but it will give you a great coping tool for your high school years.

Speaking of high school, please don't compromise yourself to make friends.

You don't need to wear that short skirt and low top to make a guy like you, and don't be willing to kiss any guy just to make you feel wanted, it doesn't work that way, that emptiness of being rejected over your looks, your parents, your religion, only gets worse when you start losing yourself and doing things that make you feel uncomfortable.

You need to have self respect and love yourself for who you are, and learn to listen to that voice in your head guiding you, it will never steer you wrong.

Many wonderful things are going to happen to you when you reach sixteen years old and you are in for a crazy few years of adventures and new experiences.

You are going to do a lot of dumb things that you will beat yourself up over, again and again until you reach your thirtie's and you realise that all the bad behaviour and wrong choices all stem from your restricted childhood and from being bullied for every single day for thirteen years, and this you will come to realise is what has made you stronger.

The mistakes you will make are not yours or anyone else's fault, it is just experience.

The strength and courage will be what you use to inspire change in others, and will find a whole new reason for being and your thirty's will be your best years yet.

There are so many positive changes coming your way, just buckle in and enjoy the ride.

You will be ok I promise, you are loved and you are wanted, you will find out who you are and you will be so proud of the woman you have become, and for that you couldn't have asked for a better life.

You will no longer be the lost little girl, you will be a strong, independent, loving woman who will inspire and teach others to not be lost children either.

I love you little girl, for who you were then, who you are now and who you will become.

Written by Monique (aged in her thirtie's)

Elise's story

I started getting teased at a very young age, it started with my own family.

My uncle and brother would say things jokingly about my weight, but when I started middle school, that is when it really began.

I was unpopular, weird, awkward and overweight, I had about three friends and I just wanted to be liked and accepted, just like everyone else, I just wanted to be happy, and I remember being called fat a lot.

There was this one guy at school in my science class who sat diagonally from me, and one of the most popular girls in school sat across from me, I used to stare at her because I was transfixed by her beauty and confidence, and I wanted to be like her.

One day she said to me can you just stop staring at me?, I got all red and looked away, and later on the guy net to her said what are you looking at you big tub of lard, and everyone laughed.

Gym class was the worst though, people would make fun of my size, my hair, my clothes and even my shoes.

One girl used to call me "free Elise" as in Free Willy the movie.

Another girl threatened to beat me up because she said I gave her friend a dirty look, which I didn't.

People were just so mean and cruel, and my siblings were ashamed of me, they were not overweight and they were both into sports, I had really come to hate myself.

About three years later I went through puberty, I got taller, lost weight and I started wearing make up, and suddenly the guys started to notice me.

I was surprised but I was happy for the first time in my life, people were admiring the way I looked rather than turning away in disgust.

I ate it all up but what I noticed happening was that I started looking for my confidence in others.

I became obsessed with having as many boyfriends as possible, they were my drug of choice, I lied to them and I said whatever I needed to if I thought they would like me more and school rarely had my focus, it was all about the boys.

Then at the age of about seventeen I tried OxyContin, between that and my boyfriend obsession, I was digging my grave fast, and at one point in 2008 my addiction to pills was so bad, I got a job as a store just so I could steal money for my habit, of course I got caught and fired and they also gave me a choice, pay back the money or face charges.

That was the turning point for me, I started calling rehabilitation Centre's, but I couldn't face my family because of the shame I felt.

This went on until Christmas Eve 2009, when my sister finally told my family, and then I went to rehab for two weeks or so and since then its been a struggle, a battle, but mostly its a choice.

I still avoid mirrors, I don't like to see myself or even hear myself, and I got pregnant in 2012 and now I have three boys, so being exposed to that has changed my outlook on life and myself.

I have a wonderful man that supports me and family that truly love me, but by no means is my life all hearts and roses.

There is so much more that I could say but this is the main hurt, I hurt myself, and my family but I'm surviving and I'm loved, ad that's more that I thought I ever deserved.

Written by Elise (aged in her thirtie's)

Mark's story

I have spent my entire life being different, if I had a dollar for every time I was called "Weird", I would be retired by now.

Being different has led to me being ostracised quite a bit, in fact for most of my life, that's why driving trucks works so well for me, I can just about completely control my environment.

I had learning disabilities when I was younger and had to take first grade twice, these days they would say I had adhd (attention deficit/ hyperactivity disorder) or something similar, but back then they called me slow.

All of this including all my sensitivities to the world and everything around it made life very difficult in my early years.

I was constantly made fun of and victimised for those difference's.

I never really had many close friends, and the ones I did have didn't stay around for too long, it got to the point where I was so desperate for friendship that I left myself open for abusive behaviour, that is until I decided I was going to go to put an end to it and pull deep inside of myself and protect myself instead.

School became hell for me, I was physically assaulted more times that I can count, treated like a less than second class citizen and ganged up on and attacked.

One time I had my clothes torn so badly in a bathroom and I was left in complete darkness half naked in there and I could hear the kids who did it laughing about it and running down the hallway.

I always got along with my teachers and that didn't get me friends either, but I had gotten to a point where I was dumbing myself down to try and fit in with the other kids, including some of the kids who had done things to me in the past, I was that desperate to fit in and make friends.

I had teachers tell me that they knew I could be so much more but that I was hanging out with the wrong crowd and I shouldn't be knocking myself down to their level.

The one bright spot happened when I was a senior, I was the only one still riding the bus to and from school in my sub division, all the other kids had cars or went back and forth with friends,

I had a friend who was a freshman who was a nice guy who also rode the bus with me, he was constantly being picked on by older kids and it brought back bad memories of a dark time for me, so I kept telling him that he needed to stand up to these guys of tell someone about it, but he was very zen and he believed he could just ignore them or he would just laugh it off.

There was one kid who was a sophomore who also rode that bus and he constantly picked on my friend everyday to school and back, it was non stop.

One day he must have hit that internal switch inside me because I had evidently had enough.

He had started picking on my friend again so I got up and confronted the kid, the bus was stopped at the last stop, the door was open, so after a few minutes of verbal sparing I realised I wasn't getting anywhere with reason and I literally picked him up and carried him to the front of the bus and I threw him out, and while he was picking himself up off the ground I said that if I saw him ever do that again I was going to get really mad.

I turned around and looked at the bus driver and I said I was sorry for what I did, she said " you have nothing to be sorry for, I wish I could have done something about him myself, and as far as I'm concerned, I didn't see a thing".

The biggest irony of this is that I got famous all over the school for it.

To this day if I see that freshman's dad he thanks me for it, the irony part is that I got a reputation as a bully for standing up to one.

Written by Mark (aged in his fiftie's)

So as you can see, you are not alone, although some of us may be viewed as old, you can see that bullying knows no age, and it has no bounds and it will affect most people in their life at one stage or another, it may not be today, it may not be tomorrow but it most probably will happen.

I'm so sorry for that, I wouldn't wish it on my worst enemy if I had one.

So next time you see someone being bullied, being picked on, being ignored, being harassed, being teased, being annoyed, know this, there are many forms of bullying and by you watching it happen, you are just as bad as the ones who do it, you are not doing anything you think?, your not responsible?

Ok now I want you to now look at it as if you were the one having all that happened to you and you see someone who feels bad for you but doesn't say anything, do you think they are just as much to blame now?

Yes you are, you have the chance to stop it, even if it's just for today, oh you think they may turn their attention on you if you try?, well guess what?, they may do that, or they may stop, you won't know until you try, you don't even have to confront them, just go tell an adult or someone in charge and let them do it, you may have just saved a life.

Maybe their life wasn't in danger at that very moment but if that continues to happen, they may decide enough is enough and try to commit suicide, or in some cases the bully has actually gone too far and killed the person they are bullying, and sometimes it's just from one punch.

Also just remember if a bully can bully anyone, they can also turn around and start bullying you, even if you help them bully, they can easily snap and turn it around on you.

So what do you think you then have to live with?, the fact you could have helped them will be with you for the rest of your life so please, if it was you being bullied you would want someone to help you, so help someone else.

You get one shot at this life, so don't spend it regretting your actions, be proud of yourself, surround yourself with caring, loving people, be a hero for someone, not because you want fame, just because you would hope someone would do it for you in that position.

CHAPTER 4

Life, learning to be a Medium

Which brings me to the here and now, well sort of, so here I was, I had just quit the job I had had at the same company for eleven years which I had loved, so I was without a job, but not really worried, I had the total support of my husband and I was finally getting to do the things I had wanted to do since becoming a mother twenty four years ago but never had the chance to do because I was raising my two children at the time on my own, so I was enjoying being a stay at home mum, I got to relax, watch my next two girls grow, I got to take them to school, and do all the things I had wanted to do for a very long time like write this book. So after job hunting for a while I decided that there was nothing that I wanted to do, nothing that required me to leave the house and missing out on my girls growing up, so I started to study online.

I started to study what interested me the most which was anything spiritual and metaphsical.

Which brought me to Erik.

Erik Medhus, he changed my life, he led me to Channeling Erik, a blog that his mother had started for Erik and his friends and family to get together in a safe environment where anyone who's interested can talk about spirit and our experiences and most of all connecting with Erik.

Erik was a young man who took his own life about 6 years ago, and then he started visiting the blog members, his family and friends from across the veil.

When people started to ask where they could get readings some of the admins of the page suggested to his mother that they open the Channeling Erik Mediums page, for anyone who connects and can channel Erik as well as any other abilities they would like to share so there was not only the Channeling Erik Facebook page, and the channelingerik.com blog, but they now had the Channeling Erik Mediums page too, which I became a member of around December 2015.

These pages as well as the mediums on them helped me to discover my own potential, and it was then that I really started to take control of my life and do what had always fascinated me, and to do what I loved most in this world, to connect with those that have crossed over.

I had been feeling numbness on my arm every time I had been thinking of spirit, of my loved ones in spirit, but I had not thought much of it, so of course I went to the doctor and asked if this may be a medical problem, because I had been diagnosed with Bell's Palsy when my third child was little, and it was a similar effect of numbness on my face I looked like I had had a stroke.

So it made me wonder, but I got a clean bill of health from my doctor and life went on, then I started hearing ringing in my ears and again went back to the doctors to rule out tintinitus or something like that, but again I was fine.

So I decided to look up my symptoms on google, which had the usual stroke for numbness, tintinitus for the ear ringing, and then something caught my attention, someone had said that when they started their "Awakening" this happened to them.

So I looked up what the heck an Awakening was and found all this other information about Awakening into the fifth dimension from the third.

So I was like okay?, Now what?

So I dug a little deeper and all of a sudden I found myself on channelingerik.com watching channeled videos of Erik's mum and a **spirit** channeler named Jamie Butler from Channeling Erik.

So I just started watching and thinking OMG yes, this is exactly what I have been looking for, my whole life I was searching for something that I knew was there but had no idea how, where or why?, It was like a light bulb finally went off in my head, and I could literally hear a sigh in the spirit world saying thank god she finally gets it.

Yes I really did finally get it, so began my epic journey into spirit.

So I joined the Channeling Erik family. Family you ask?, yes that is exactly what it has become for me and for many thousands of people from all around the world have become my family all thanks to Erik.

I first came across Erik's spirit when there was an ask Erik section on one of the blogs, Erik was being channeled by Alison Ailfinn Allan from ascendingthepath.com, and she also has a utube page called the Shiny Show, which she does with Kari Silver Lining, and they channel many different spirits, from Source to the planets, and I asked Erik and Alison a question or three and Alison would channel Erik's response, and I was so nervous waiting for a response.

I wanted to know if I was an Empath?, how I can use that to my advantage, how I could control the feelings I got around people, as I was always so overwhelmed around a big crowd.

My biggest problem I had was that I would walk into a room of people and know the mood of the room, what they had been talking about and I would feel either totally elated or totally drained in seconds, it was becoming a problem.

I would also get a headache when I was around someone, then they would say, " I have a headache", and thinking it was just a coincidence I would just brush it off, but then it would happen all the time, it was driving me crazy, from headaches to stomach aches to mood swings, if someone came in a room I was in and got angry I would get angry, and then they would feel better but I wouldn't.

I was also seeing repeating numbers all the time as well, especially 11.11 and 1.11, I would literally see them everywhere, on my phone, on my oven, on the Ipad, house numbers, trucks, cars.

The worst was and still is when my family are in a bad mood or are sick, I would immediately be in a bad mood and I would get sick feelings too until I figured out what was happening and could either help or in some cases I just had to walk away, as the feeling's I get when someone is in a bad mood can be very overwhelming for me, it can feel like I'm being hit by a 10 tonne truck.

I needed answers, and I also felt as though I was going crazy because I would have conversations in my head and my head would answer back in my own voice, it has been happening my whole life so I figured I was nuts.

Trust me I know there was more than my fair share of people who agreed with me there.

So with all these things in mind I finally got up courage to get the question answered by Erik, and he confirmed through Alison so much for me, it literally changed my life.

So the next step for me was to get a reading done by Alison too, and would you believe I was so nervous I had butterflies all morning waiting for the reading, I spent about half an hour beforehand sitting on my bed just trying to calm my heart.

Then finally it happened and Alison asked me if I was nervous because Erik had shown up in my reading and told her I had been panicking right before the reading, nothing is sacred when spirit are around, they see all.

I was by myself that day so there was no way she could have known that I was nervous because I didn't show it when we started and she couldn't have found out by anyone so I knew she got the information from Erik.

She immediately made me feel at ease saying that Erik said I wasn't just an Empath, I was very Empathic and that I was not going crazy, and that I have been channeling my whole life, and he had high hopes that I would be channeling for him and with him for his erikmedhusdownunda.com blog, I was like what?, How? I can't do what Alison does, but he said I will.

He told me to meditate regularly and to protect myself, which was necessary at the time considering I was worried about what may try and come in while I'm open to spirit, I was not really sure at this stage what was true and what wasn't regarding spirits as I had been brought up partly Catholic.

My Maternal grandmother was the first of my loved ones to come through for me, even though I didn't ask for her as we hadn't been close in life, but never the less she came through to tell me she is now my gatekeeper in spirit.

Well this is when I found out that it doesn't matter how your relationship was in life, when you go back home to spirit everything changes, you are no longer able to hold onto ego, and you are all about love.

Also you can see once your in spirit, your soul groups, your connections to all your incarnations right from the beginning of your soul being created, time is not linear there like it is on earth so everything is happening all at once.

My grandmother and I in spirit have history, she told me that I come from a long line of healers and that I have been a healer in all of my past lives in one way or another, for example in the 1800's I was an animal healer, and in the times of the Native Indian's I was a medicine man, among many other past lives.

My grandmother is in my close soul group, the closest people in spirit for me when I'm in spirit too.

Which brings me to Higher Selves, we each have a Higher Self in spirit, every single person on earth has a Higher Self.

When a spirit wants to learn something they will split off a part of themselves along with parts of other to make you, then the spirit (you) picks the life they want, the parents they want, etc etc and this is your soul contract which is all part of your incarnation.

You set out all the things you want to accomplish and how you want to do it, and who you want to do it with, you pick our your guides or they choose to help you of their own free will, and then your ready to go into the human you picked to be your mother, and then you become the baby that Is born to them.

Your life then begins, you may be born to someone who plans on giving you up for adoption, you already know this and you chose to incarnate to them anyway because this will lead you to the life you are wanting to lead, or you may choose to live happily with only one parent, or with the same sex couple as your parents, either way you chose this and you knew what was going to happen before you chose the incarnation even if the parent had no idea what would happen except on a soul level, but you know what will **happen.**

Part of you is still in spirit (your Higher Self) and there are often other incarnations of yourself on earth too, just experiencing a different life that you are or even a very similar life as you are, these are called parallel lives, the life you have now on earth is called your Lower Self.

Also many spirits choose not to go into the body of the foetus until it's born, they hang out on the mothers side of her body until the baby is born, I have seen this with my own eyes too many times to count, and I know your thinking how is the baby alive then if it has no soul inside?, well from what I have learnt from my own son's in spirit, until I could see for myself is that they are still connected to the body of the child, and the body can still survive in utero until the baby is born, its similar to when someone is in a coma, their body is still alive but it seems like no one is home, often the soul may be still connected to the body just hanging around outside of it until they either pass away or come back into the body and wake up again.

I know there are many people out there who have lost their babies in utero, including myself five times, and want to reassure you that your babies are always with you, they are not actually babies unless they chose to be, which they can certainly do if they choose to, they are evolved souls, they chose you to be their mother and they knew that they would not be making it to birth when they decided to experience life either inside your baby or outside your baby, either way they will always be our baby.

Some people believe that abortion is a sin in the eyes of God, well let me tell you what I know, in my experience with spirit and especially with my own son, it's just not true.

These spirits choose to experience this, like I said time is not linear there, so they know exactly what they are getting into, even though you may not, and it doesn't matter how the child was conceived either, there is no judgement, there is not punishment, there is only love and only experience, there may be a very good reason why this has happened to the person, as it may be a turning point in their lives where they will then help others who have lost babies, or have aborted their babies, or who have been raped, and felt they had no other choice so they choose to help others like them, there is always a reason, and the only punishment they will get is what they give themselves, and what other humans decide to give them, in spirit they only love you and would never like to see you hurting.

Your baby (evolved spirit) loves you so much that they wanted to help you experience this in your life, you may not think you had a choice, you may have done it for your own reasons, either way they knew what they were getting into and they don't judge you, in fact they wanted to experience this too for whatever reason and they wanted to help your spirit evolve as well as their own by helping you experience it.

Please never feel guilty for something you felt was necessary at the time, this was part of your life plan, for your own soul's evolvement, maybe you would become the best mother ever because of that experience because of what you went through, or maybe you become and advocate for rape victims, or maybe you start a support group for other mothers in the same position?, whatever the reason this is something you planned before you incarnated.

Please do not get me wrong here, I am not an advocate for abortion especially when you are just being sloppy with protecting yourself, or if your not in a position to have a child, its better in this day and age to protect yourself first, then if it happens anyway and you absolutely are not in a position to have a child, then do what you feel is right for you, I believe in all people choosing for themselves their own journey, but please think before you act, always get protection if you can't have a child right now.

Also remember that this is only my opinion on the subject, not what spirit feels, or what God feels, they do not punish or judge you, only humans do that, but I do want you to think before you act, for your own well being.

Also if this was something that came from no fault of your own, know that I understand, I really do understand and I know some of you will do what you need to do, so please, again do not feel guilty, this is part of your souls journey.

Since time is not linear in spirit we are able to experience our past, present/parallel and future lives all at the same time and sometimes you may choose to split off and incarnate more that one soul, you may choose for example to incarnate a few or more souls at once, personally the most parallel lives I have seen one person have was three, but that doesn't mean there are not people who have more, anything is possible.

Remember again that time is not linear in spirit so everything is happening right now, your past, your future and your present is all happening right now, all at once so every time you learn something new or evolve in your thinking it changes your past, future and present.

It's a fascinating process really, to learn about something that is so out of our way of thinking, we have learnt our whole lives that the past is fixed, the future hasn't happened yet and suicides and people who do bad things go to hell.

Boy do we all have a rude awakening when we all cross over.

Which then brings me to my beautiful boys in spirit, Matthew and Neil, they were miscarriages I had, I had lost Neil when I was about four months pregnant when I was around twenty four years old, and I lost Matthew only about six years ago.

I had thought about Neil my whole life, I don't think we ever forget the babies we lose, it felt to me like a ripple effect in my life, it really hurt but at the time I was also relieved and I felt so guilty about that for a very long time.

I know it sounds mean to think that way about him, but ill be honest, it was how I felt, I had very mixed up feelings at the time.

I don't regret anything in my life now, everything that has happened in my life up to now because these were my life lessons to learn, and don't get me wrong, I loved that boy more than anything, however he chose not to incarnate as was his choice, just as it was just as much mine, and the first thing he said to me was don't feel guilty for not wanting me mum, I chose not to incarnate this time around but to watch over you from spirit instead, it was a lesson for us both.

Did this make me feel less guilty?, hmmm maybe a little but not much, I still felt like I should have wanted him, and it's not that I didn't really want him, it was just not the ideal situation to bring up another child in as I already had a daughter, but I would have, with out a doubt I would have and I had every intention of keeping him, but I lost him.

We come into this life with our lessons to learn and experiences to experience, and no one and nothing can experience them for us, its something we must go through on our own, we can share our journey with other people but ultimately its our experiences and our lives to live.

Don't let anyone make decisions for you, be who and what you want to be, do what makes your heart happy, not your head.

We start out life doing what our parents, teachers, friends etc want us to be and do, but once we are finished with school and ready to adult then its up to us to decide what it is we will be doing for the rest of our lives, not anyone else, they don't walk in our shoes, they can't control us, only themselves, and we need to enjoy this life and do what we set out to do before we incarnated, however do it in a way that doesn't hurt or make other people feel bad, most parents for example love and want what is best for us/you, and most have brought you up with the values and lessons they were taught, so don't hate them for that, just respect their decisions, and respect the fact that they have done everything in their power so you can be who you are meant to be, even though it may not be what you plan for yourself, just thank them for giving you life, and for giving you everything they could with the knowledge they had and then forgive them and let them know that you have your own plan for your own life.

If they don't understand then that's ok, they don't need to right now, but if you decide to take your own course in your life then expect to do it with or without the support, with or without the cozy room you have at your parents house, you may have to do it alone, even with your families support and you need to be ready to stand on your own two feet, now I'm talking about those over the age of eighteen, if your not over the age of eighteen but have found yourself in a situation where you have to leave home, or you don't have any support around you, then there are support groups, and people who can help you get on your feet, this is more directed at the adults that have just come into their own and want to draw a path for themselves, however please don't think you are alone, or that you're not important enough, you are, I have been you, I was kicked out of home at the age of fifteen, and if it wasn't for a beautiful young lady named Nadja, I don't think I would have survived, she was my earth angel, she took me in, and she changed my life, so if you don't find anyone like that to help you, just know that your guides are not going to leave you hanging, they will point you in the direction you need to go to fulfil your own purpose, and if that means going to a friends house, or living on the streets there is always a reason, you may decide to help street kids in your future, or run a soup kitchen, there is always a reason and its what you have chosen for yourself.

We chose our life, we chose our parents and we chose to experience what we experience for the growth of our souls, the good, the bad and the ugly.

People that hurt us, and teach us, whether its to be strong or to love more, or to love less, or it may be to leave the people around us that do these things to us, whether its abuse, personality clash, or any other reason, either way, every experience teaches us something, and its something we may know at the time, or it may be something that we don't learn until we are much older, or it may be something only our **soul k**nows, either way I like to say, acknowledge what has happened, mourn it if you feel you need to, then kiss it goodbye and send it away, try not to let it control you, try not to let it take over your life and your happiness, we all deserve to be happy no matter what we have chosen for our lives, we all deserve it!

So back to my beautiful boys, Matthew likes to hang out with my husband Leighton, and my two youngest daughter's (his dad and his sisters), he loves to go to work with my husband, he loves the beach, and loves to play with the girls.

My son Neil likes to hang out with me, he has followed me through my life since the day he died, he has grown as he would if he had survived, he'd around twenty one years old, sometimes he comes to me as a small child, and sometimes he comes in as a teenager, but mostly he comes in as the age he would have been had he lived.

He tells me that we have had many lives together, he has been my father in many lives and I have been his mother in many lives too, among other things like being friends, enemies, strangers, etc, he is in my close knit soul group so we have experienced many lives together.

On occasion my son, my grandmother and Erik all come in together to talk to me, sometimes its just each of them on their own, sometimes its others too.

My most favourite memory of my son is when one night I was in bed waiting for my husband to get home, our kids were in bed and I was just laying there talking to my son and asking him to sit with me while I waited for my husband to come home, he very clearly said, "I'm here mum, I'll stay here until dad gets home" and I just smiled because it was the first time I heard him with my ears and not telepathically, it was amazing to me that it was my son that chose to talk to me that way and not anyone else because it made it all the more special for me, I also saw him clearly too, he touched me on my back which I also felt, and I saw and indent on the bed where he sat, it was the most beautiful moment in my life.

I want anyone who has lost a child, whether it be by miscarriage, abortion, or as a living breathing child or adult of theirs to know that your kids adore you, they love you so much, they will watch over you and send you signs, which I will go into further into the book, but please know this, if you know nothing else, they love you more than you will ever know, and they are with you the second you think about them.

They are with you, comforting you when you are sad about them, but most of all I want you to know that they are not in pain, they did not feel pain when they died, and that goes for any way they died, unless they chose to experience pain for their own spiritual growth, but that is rare, normally their guides, loved ones and angels take them from their body before they feel anything that will cause them pain.

Please know that they are not hurting, and all they want from you is for you to love and remember them as they were, it does not matter if the only memory you have was seeing that pregnancy test with two lines, or if you spent many many years with them, they love you more than they could ever possibly explain and they just want you to be happy.

Now just to clarify my husband isn't my son Neil's father, my eldest child's father was but the fact that he chose to call him dad meant so much to me.

I also want to tell you about my other son Matthew too, he is my husbands child, we miscarried him just before we fell pregnant with our last child Ella, he is a part of my husbands soul group, and he prefers to spend more time with them rather than me, not because he doesn't love me, but because he chose to come in as their guide.

I love him just as much as my other children, he is watched over by my son Neil and my grandmother, but he is an evolved soul too, and even though he comes to us as a six year old, he is a very smart evolved soul.

My son Matthew is not part of my inner soul group and neither is my husband, but that doesn't mean we love each other less, or that we wouldn't do anything for each other, we are soul mates not twin flames and I could not have picked a more perfect person for me if I had tried, so don't judge a book by its cover, go with what's in your heart and it will never lead you wrong.

CHAPTER 5

Follow your heart

Now I'm going to tell you about the time that changed my life forever, I touched on it at the beginning of the book, remember the dream I had when I was about 7 years old, and I was asleep in bed, in my room at home, I remember waking up to see a portal on the wall next to my bed.

I felt feelings of overwhelming love, I wasn't scared at all, I remember seeing two beings, a male and a female, and I felt they were my real parents, or at least they presented themselves that way as I was just a child, and they were the most beautiful beings I had ever seen in my life, they were glowing, they looked like Aliens to me, now looking back I know they were pleadians, but I just thought they looked beautiful and loving.

They were telling me that what I was seeing was my home, and that when I was done with this incarnation I would be back in their loving arms, and I wanted so bad to go through that portal and just stay there forever, but they told me I couldn't go in as a human, I wouldn't survive it, and that I was needed here for when I became an adult.

I didn't understand anything other than I was done with my family on earth and I was ready to go where they were, but they wouldn't let me so I started crying, then screaming, I felt betrayed because they had said I could go home but then they wouldn't let me go there.

In my 7 year old mind I was gutted, all I wanted was to go home, they then told me how much they loved me and how they were so proud of me, and that I would grow up to do great things, and then they were gone.

I found out many years later that my soul is from a star/planet called Andromeda Nebulas, I don't know much about it, but when I heard that I knew it was right, and that was the beautiful place I saw that night.

I thought I was going nuts for a long time, everyone thought Aliens didn't exist, and that Ghosts, Spirits, fairies and other beings were not real, so I had a hard time growing up when I knew these things were real.

My father started to shake me thinking I was having a nightmare because of all the screaming and crying, and he said that when he looked in my eyes they looked as though I was looking through him not at him.

The next time I was taken to church or had religious instruction (RI) at school, everything they said no longer felt right to me, especially when they said things like that all children should be christened or they will go to hell, or when they said be good always but if your not confess your sins or you will go to hell.

None of this made any sense to me so I asked my RI teacher what if babies died before they got christened, would they still go to hell, I meant what if they were about to get christened but died before they could, and she said no, I don't think so, that would be the parents sin.

So then I said what if your parents didn't believe in Church and didn't want to get them christened?, and she couldn't give me an answer because she didn't know.

From then on I was asking question's all the time and the answers never felt true to me, so as I got older I started looking at different religions, I was trying to make sense of the feeling I felt that God was real, but not in the way people thought.

To me it felt like he was a Source of power, something a part of me, not separate from me, not some man that watches everything we do with judgement, not some man saying right you drank alcohol, or snuck out to a party, or swore, or whatever else people think we should be judged for, and then says ok your going to hell, but if you say your sorry you can go to heaven again.

I felt like I was a part of it, and it was a part of me, I felt he/she was the creator of all things, that we are put on earth by our own doing, not out of punishment and that its all a stage and we were playing our parts for ourselves not for others.

I spoke to Source years later and I asked him/her the question, do you punish us?

This is what he/she said, "Why would I punish you?, you are a part of me, why would I punish myself? If I was to punish you I would feel that punishment myself, why would I want to feel that, when I can feel your love and your happiness?

So this was all put on the back burner and brought up on occasion when someone mentioned it, or when a lovely couple tried to sway me to become a Jehovah Witness, don't get me wrong, I really liked this couple, and because I liked them I tried it out, once only to find it was more of the same things just reworded.

I really had hoped I would find my place in this world, and they made me feel very welcome, but it wasn't for me.

The next time I saw them, the wife was with her adult daughter and grandchildren, they had somehow managed to knock on my door again but I had moved five hours away in a new town, in a new house, so I thought this is not a coincidence.

I felt I was meant to know her husband had died, and that she was still waiting for the sign they had promised each other for when one of them passed.

She got me thinking about signs from loved ones on the other side, I wondered if they could give us signs, and I came to the conclusion that not only was It probable that they could give signs but most likely possible.

I had read so many medium books, but now I was taking more notice, I started reading more, and learning more, I believed I was meant to see that lady and her family again so I could be led in this direction, I just didn't know it at that moment, but I knew it wasn't a coincidence.

I decided I would look up becoming a hairdresser when I was nineteen, I had just had my first child and I had wanted to make something of myself, and I wanted people to stop looking at me like my life was over because I was a single mum, I wanted to stand on my own two feet.

So off I went and learning about spirituality went on the back burner while I went to get a career.

So by the time my daughter was three, I was working full time in a hairdressing salon and working weekends at the local market doing hair wraps, so seven days a week I was working and I barely had time for my daughter not alone anything else.

Then one day I just had enough of hairdressing and I decided to try something else after deciding to completely change my life.

So when my daughter was almost 5, I started at a different company and completely change my life.

I started at a company that made canopies for Ute's, and Ute lids, I was their delivery driver, and I fell in love with being out on the road six days a week, and life had become great, and then I was promoted to their Sales Rep and I enjoyed travelling all over the country.

I had re met an old friend and crush I had met when my daughter was a baby and now she was six years old and we rekindled our friendship and had a daughter together, then we married and I quit my job to be a full time mum.

We grew apart quite fast, no ones fault, these things just happen ad so I was back to square one, no job, no career and now I had two daughters to support on my own.

So I got back up after a really hard time of being down, and by the time my youngest daughter was almost five and my eldest was twelve we had moved five hours away, and it was the start of a new life and I got back into hairdressing.

So we spent the next five years there, and life had many interesting twists and turns as I had decided hairdressing wasn't for me, I got tired of being treated like the dirt under peoples feet and yet still expected to be a psychotherapist, therapist, listener, punching bag among many other things, so off I went again to find a place I belonged.

The place I got a job at, they were looking for a man but I went for it anyway and I managed to get the job.

I worked there for a few years until I met my husband number two and moved back to Adelaide and moved in with him and started my life over again.

This is where my life starts to get really good.

We were together for three months when we found out that we were expecting baby number three for me and number five for him, and out came another daughter and we married a year later and four years later I fell pregnant with my fourth and last daughter and we became a bigger family than the Brady Bunch.

Life is great, amazing even, in between pregnancies and a wedding I had started with the same company, I had transferred over to the one in Adelaide when I moved back here.

So all in all I spent eleven years with that company until I got tired of the bullying and threats that were subtle but there to manipulate and to keep me under the thumb, after being happy with that company all those years, the last few months were hell.

It's not ok for bosses to treat you like that, and I chose not to let him, so I left, without a backwards glance, my time with that company was over, even though I adored my job, I mean how many people actually love their job?, so that is what really made me sad, that a bully was given the position of power and he treated everyone, not just me, like we were poo under his shoe and that there is no one better than him.

He lost and fired many great workers that had been there for years, and that is just not right, I'm glad I left, but other really good workers there did not get that chance, and I feel that putting a bully in a position to do that says a lot for the company, and a lot about him.

My advice, never ever let anyone bully you, especially when you do you job well and with love, but not at anytime.

Once his bosses realised the kind of boss and man he was he should have been taken out of the company but they didn't so he continues to bully over that place and he has now lost every person that was there when I was there, except one, and even other people in other sections left because of him, and I know also that business is not good there either so they should have listened to the workers that had been there for years who were making the company strive, and instead they have a bully who will run the place into the ground.

We all deserve to be treated with respect, and no one deserves to be treated as we did.

So now I was home full time, being a mum, life was great, my eldest daughter had left home and gotten married and now had two beautiful daughters of her own, and I was enjoying staying at home and being a full time mum and doing my readings.

My favourite subject is past lives, I kind of fell into it but its been an amazing experience reading other people's past life experiences, and I have done hundreds and hundreds of them, and its still so fascinating to me, because I never know what I'm going to see until I see it.

I literally see it like a movie in my head, it's like I'm there as a bystander just watching what's going on and relaying it to paper, I usually get their first name and I can see what they look like so I can draw them too if the client would like me too.

I call myself and Intuitive Medium, but I have all the Clairs, just my strongest is my intuition.

When I first found out that I could talk to spirit mostly it was intuitively, but since then my abilities have grown so much and I have many more now.

List of Abilities

Clairaudient – meaning you can hear voices inside your mind (telepathically) or you can hear them like a person talking to you, your more of a listener than a talker, connect with animals and plants, you may have experienced your ears ringing or a buzzing in your ears too.

Clairvoyant – You dream a lot, daydream a lot, or have a very active imagination, can see shapes, colours that others may not see, or when your meditating you can see like a movie playing in your head, see sparkly lights and or flashes of light or even movement out of the corner of your eyes to realise nothing is actually there.

Clairsentience – Clear feeling, the ability to feel strong emotion of others, be it human, animal, plants or spirit, you can feel with your heart and with your body and you can feel spirits around you too.

This is also what is known as an Empath.

You can walk into a room and feel the vibe of what's going on around you, even if no one is in the room, but may have been in there before.

For example people may have been arguing in the room a few minutes before you walked in and then they walked out and you walked in and you could feel the tension radiating the room.

You may find it very difficult going into crowded places, you may suddenly feel upset, tense, feeling like you just want to run home as fast as you can.

You may see a friend and instantly know how she/he is feeling without them saying a word.

Sometimes people also feel others pain, like often I will get headaches out of nowhere and suddenly someone near me will say they have had a headache all day.

Claircognizance – Clear Knowing

This was one of my first and still is one of my strongest abilities, the ability to just know that something is right or wrong, it's just a clear knowing without a doubt what is going on around you.

For example your partner says he went to work, but you just know he went to the beach instead, you have no idea how you know but you just know he/she is lying.

You may have a very busy mind, you may have constant thoughts rolling around in your head to the point that you can't sleep because you just can't seem to quiet your mind.

You may have creative ideas that just need to be done right now, even though you may not enjoy creative things, to find that you are channeling something from spirit.

Most people have one or more of these abilities and may not even realise it, or if your like me you may have been thinking all your life that you were going nuts, well I'm here to tell you, you are most likely not going crazy.

I do like to say though, always get a doctor to give you a clean bill of health first, just to be sure and then you can move forward into developing your abilities.

Other less known about Clairs include.

Clairscent

Is to smell a fragrance/odour of a substance like food, smelly socks, roses which is not in your surrounding.

You can smell them without the aid of your nose, they seem to just appear in my experience, its like a knowing to me, I know I am smelling roses, and I know for a fact there are no roses around.

Clairtangency

Is a clear touching or more commonly known as psychometry.

Its when you hold or touch an object and can see or feel information about the object about its owner or history that will not have been known before by the person touching or holding the object.

Clairgustance

Is one I don't particular like much, just like clairscent you are perceiving something that is not physically there, you can taste something that isn't in or hasn't been in your mouth.

You are getting the information from spirit, it may have been grandmas favourite pudding, and grandma has been gone a long time and she wanted to remind you that she is with you, so she lets you taste the pudding.

Every single person in the world has them, it's just a matter of studying them, working out what you resonate with and what else you would like to learn, if your intention is to be a medium or psychic for example, then study, find a mentor, you can do it just like anything else you may want to learn.

I believe in you, and I know you can do it if it's what you want to do.

I can hear you saying "But what if everyone thinks I'm crazy?", well that is a great question, and one that I know others have asked and are still asking themselves, as well as myself at the beginning of my journey.

Here is my answer, who cares?, I mean really, who cares?, your mum and dad?, your religious aunt?, who?

Will they tell you to go away and not come back?, will that bother you?

I can tell you this, if they don't support your decision which they may not, what is the worst that can happen?

Personally I think if they don't accept you for who you are, or if they don't love you for who you are, then they don't deserve to be a part of your life.

This, I learnt the hard way, and I don't want any of you to have to experience that, so if you think it's going to be a problem then talk it out with them first, if you feel you need to get their approval, if you don't then go for it, what will be will be, but in the end, you will be happy and that is all that matters.

Many people who are famous were told they couldn't do it, or shouldn't do it, whatever they had chosen to do, some came from a family of doctors, lawyers etc who wanted their children to follow in their footsteps, but instead they followed their hearts and their dreams, and if they hadn't done that, they would never have entertained us, or enjoyed what they achieved. So always follow your heart, this is what you came here wanting to do, why would you fight that or let someone take that away from you?

I say go for it, no matter what it is you want, do it, you only get one shot at this life to follow your heart and dreams so why wouldn't you?

Now I want to talk about equality, do I believe in it? Yes without a doubt.

I believe everyone in this world deserves to have a chance at a happy life, whether they are gay, straight, black, white, red or blue, whether they are religious, not religious at all, or spiritual, or whatever, I think they deserve to be happy, if that means gay partners want to marry they should be able to, if a black and white couple want to marry the should be able to, if they want to adopt a interracial child let them, as long as no one is getting hurt or abused in any way who are we to judge? Who gave anyone permission to say I speak for God? No one!

Only God/Source can speak for himself, we are all God/Source so we all get to decide what we want for ourselves, but you don't get to decide or tell other people what they can or can't do.

This is not the middle ages, this is 2017 and we have all got to the point that we don't care what other people think or say about us, its our life, its our journey so live it.

Telling someone they are an abomination in the eyes of the lord because they want to marry their same sex partner says more about you as a human than it ever will about the two people who adore each other and want to spend the rest of their lives together, it says that you are so unhappy with your life and your own restrictions that you don't want anyone else to be happy.

Grow up people, we are heading into a new age of love, and those that live for hate, violence, fascism, racism, and the list goes on will be surrounded by love and there will be no where to go but into love.

I'm not saying you have to love, but life can be so much nicer if you do.

The only way you can love someone else properly is by loving yourself properly first, then you will know what it is you want from others and you will find like minded people.

When you don't love or even like yourself you can and usually do attract the same type of people to you, the ones that get you in troubling situations, that you may never recover from, you may end up in jail, or on the streets, anything is possible really and that goes both ways, whether good or bad.

So work out what you want, and go and get it, even if its as simple as a friend, you don't have to change yourself for others to like you, change so that you can like and even love you, and then the right people will be the ones you attract, its call the law of attraction.

CHAPTER 6

Meditation and Believing in Yourself

Believing in yourself and loving who you are may be one of the hardest things you will ever have to do.

To love yourself is to know who you are and to be proud of who you are, it doesn't matter what other people think of you, it only matters what you think of yourself, easy for me to say? Yes it is now actually, but it wasn't always, I went through primary school and parts of high school being told I wasn't good enough.

I wasn't pretty enough, I wasn't fat enough, I was a stick, ugly, prudish, my family wasn't rich enough, around enough, around too much, it seemed there was nothing about me that anyone liked, and it had me in tears too many times to count.

It made me feel worthless at the time, I had one friend in primary school at the time, and everyone was pretty much mean and nasty, or they just ignored me.

I watched my children go through the same things and its just not right, we are all different, and we are all different for a reason, if we all looked the same we would look very silly and no one could tell the difference between anyone because there would be none.

I want each and every one of you to stand in front of a mirror and have a really good look at yourself, I want you to know you are very beautiful and this stage, whatever stage your at in your life will not last, so enjoy it, embrace it, love yourself for who you are and for who you will become, because you are beautiful inside and out.

If you look in that mirror and see someone who is a bully, nasty, mean to other people, then ask yourself what it is you can do to change that?

Be nicer to your parents?, be nicer to the kids at school who sit alone at lunch looking sad?

Whatever it is you see, change it, if you don't like who you are becoming, change it, you are the only person other than your guides who can change you, if they see you going down the wrong path, they will put a road block in your way, and you will learn what it is you need to learn, now I don't want you to freak out and say omg I'm going to hell, because there is no hell except the one you make for yourself.

As I have said a few times now, there is no punishment, there is no karma, only lessons and love and we learn best by love and not fear.

Fear is the very first thing you need to get rid of, it does you no good to fear anything, just change it.

One of my children has been bullied for a fair whack of her school years, I asked my Higher Self why that is happening to my sweet girl who just wants only for everyone to love each other and be nice to one another, and she said, that in her last life she was the bully and in this life she chose to know what it felt like, and it would help shape her into the kind, beautiful, loving woman she will become, by being bullied, you see the bad side, but it also makes you long for the good stuff too, so although people would call this karma, its more about lessons, it was her choice, not a punishment, not paybacks just her choice to learn from it, as is all your choices you make, you make those decisions for your own spiritual growth.

Everything you learn as the human being you are, your Higher Self learns, they experience what you experience, the good, the bad and the ugly.

There is a lot of controversy over karma, and I know some people

71

will have their own strong opinions on it, but I got my opinions and truth from spirit, this is something they have already experienced, so why not go straight to the source.

And its your all about spiritual growth, not punishment.

So if your a bully right now in your life, remember its quite possible that you may choose to come back next time and be the one that's bullied, so think about that when you look in the mirror.

It does not matter if you are large, small, a red head, a brunette or a blonde, smart, or not as smart yet, these are all things you can either love about yourself or change, if you want to change it, do it for you, not for anyone else, do it because you feel you will be happier if you do.

I have seen the caterpillar that grew up to be a butterfly, I was one of them, and did it change me as a person? Maybe for a while yes, but I always found something else I wasn't happy with.

Until I looked in that mirror and said I'm perfect just the way I am without worrying about what other people thought of me I wasn't really here, I was just playing a role of who everyone else wanted me to be, and you know what?, no matter what I did, I couldn't make them happy, even my own parents walked away from me anyway.

I don't feel sorry for myself, because I have a wonderfully supportive husband who loves me just the way I am, and I don't have to change for him, and I have 4 wonderful children, and two wonderful grandchildren and some wonderfully supportive friends who have always stood by me, so if anyone else doesn't accept me, then that's ok, I have made peace with myself.

The sooner everyone makes peace with who they are the sooner you can't be hurt by others, its not putting a barrier up so no one can get close its letting things brush over you not letting fear rule your life, remember my favourite quote?

People project onto others what they are insecure of in themselves, people call others fat, because they are afraid of getting fat themselves, people say others are ugly because they are afraid others see them as ugly.

Don't let other people's fear rule you, and don't let your own rule you.

People often are afraid of spirits, they think if you mess with the spirit world you will bring evil into your life, so they pull out bible quotes and believe they are right.

Each and every human alive are spirits, they were spirits before and they will be spirits again, so if we are spirits what are you afraid of?, Yourself?

We are spirits having a human experience.

So every time you ask a question and the answer pops in your head, where do you think that came from?, it comes from your Higher Self, who is a spirit, you are just a small part of them here to experience life.

It's funny really because many people think that if you can't see it, hear it, smell it etc then its not real, it can't exist, yet they wholeheartedly believe in God, they put their who trust in someone they have never met, seen, heard etc but they wont trust that other things may be real too like UFO's, Aliens, Fairies, Dragon's and other mythical things.

They follow a book that Jesus himself said was misconstrued by humans to control the masses, yet many people will still fight in Gods name.

We are created from source (God) then we each come here and live lives so we can evolve in spirit, everything we experience, source experiences, so why oh why would God choose to punish himself?

When you think by doing something wrong you will go to hell, you are letting fear rule your life, which is exactly what the people who rewrote the bible had intended, they wanted it changed to scare people into doing the right thing.

I know for a fact there will be people who read this book and say that I'm probably possessed by they devil, and the devil is making me say it, well I'm sorry to disappoint you but the devil doesn't exist, Lucifer however is actually a really great spirit to talk to, you should try having a conversation with him, he is really not what the masses have made you believe about him.

So me being evil is so far from the truth, but people will believe what they want to believe and that is their choice and their opinion and I would never try and make them believe in what I believe, that is their belief system and they have a right to it, its wrong but that's only in my opinion, and in my experience.

I get my information directly from Source, the Source of all things and so I will trust him/her before I trust a book that was written by man many many years ago.

When you get your information straight from Source you get the facts, anyone can get them, just close your eyes, ask the question and see what information you can get, you may be very surprised because every single person in the world has access to this information, its not given only if you have a "Gift" because it is not a Gift" its an ability and each ability can be accessed by anyone who wants to use it, so give it a try.

Anyway what people think about me is none of my business so I will keep doing what I do, and others can continue what they do, we all come into our own truth in time, one way or another so its only a matter of time.

Just know you are loved, your loved ones in spirit adore you, they are with you the second you think about them, just close your eyes, sit quietly and talk to them, you can speak out loud or you can do it in your head (telepathically), it doesn't matter how you do it because they will hear you either way, then just listen to what they have to say, I guarantee you are going to feel love and hear nothing but love.

They want nothing more than for you to be happy, and sometimes they will give you a little nudge in the right direction to find that happiness.

That's how I found my husband, in 2007 I lived five hours away from him, we both went on a dating site and for some strange reason his picture just kept coming up all the time, and after seeing it over and over and over again many times a day for many days I just threw my hands up and said ok, I give up, I get it, you want me to meet him.

I wasn't going to be the one to make the first move so if he messaged me first then I knew it was meant to be, so then he messages me out of the blue, so we talked and then I found out my picture kept coming up too for him, and then a few months after we started talking we met, and once we met I knew in that very second that he was the one I was going to spend the rest of my life with, I heard in my head, "He is the one you will marry".

We married in 2009 when our daughter was one year old, and three years after that had our last daughter.

We have now been together ten years in February and we have been married eight years this year.

So spirit can help you find your soul mate, they can also give you signs that they aren't the one, just listen to your body, listen to your stomach, do you feel sick when you meet someone, do you get a strange feeling in your stomach?, this is a warning, this is your guides letting you know that if you continue with a relationship with this person it will not work.

Just know that you are using your free will if you decide to go ahead anyway, I felt that feeling many times in my life, in a way I'm glad I didn't listen but sometimes I wish I had, so just listen to your body and your feelings, if it feels good like butterflies, its a good thing, if it feels like a yucky stomach ache then its your warning.

If you meditate on your question's you will find that you will get a clear answer way before you make the decision and it will help guide you into making good decisions.

Now learning to meditate can be easy for some people and very difficult for others, but its really really good for your state of mind and not to mention your mental health, it gives you time to yourself with no interruptions and if you make it a regular thing in your week you can spend time with spirit, whether it will be your spirit guides, your angels, your loved one or just a spirit wanting help, or you may also encounter, a spirit animal, fairies, dragons, and so many other beings its literally limitless.

I know it can be very difficult for those who have such a busy mind that literally keep's going all day and night, I know because I was that person, I was that person who couldn't sleep at night, couldn't sit quietly, I had to keep my mind busy at all times, so when Erik told me I needed to start meditating I was like um ok, I have tried before but its so hard to not let my mind wander so what can I do to help that?

He told me to try the guided meditations instead of just the music, he said it would give me something to focus on, so I tried and it really did help.

I started dong meditations three times a week, I did two lots of twenty minute guided meditations in succession (one right after the other) and the more I did it the quieter my mind became during the day and at night, I started sleeping better, I felt generally better so I upped them to daily, and then I found my connection with spirit was becoming much stronger too, and gradually my abilities grew more and more each day with new experiences all the time.

I went back to three times a week though because I found it was just too hard for me to fit it in seven days a week, but if I could have I would have, even if it was just twenty minutes a day instead of fourty, but when your working eight hours a day, sometimes more and have three children at home, it can be very difficult.

Some people like to do a five to ten minute meditation every day before they start their day, others like to listen to it at night when they go to sleep, others do it when they feel like it, and honestly there is no right or wrong way, its just what works for you.

Meditation should be relaxing, enjoyable and comfortable for you so if your getting headaches, or your uncomfortable etc then maybe start off slow, some people have told me that everytime they try and meditate their head feels like its going to explode, it may be your third eye opening up, or it could be something totally unrelated but either way it shouldn't be like that, not to the point that you get a migraine for the rest of the day, its supposed to be relaxing, a little pressure on your third eye is normal but migraines are not.

There are many different types of meditations so ill give you a few different types to try, my favourites are Kundalini, binaural beats (but I only like to do these occasionally because they can mess with my mind), guided meditations, (because I still like to have something to focus on) ad Chakra cleansing meditations because I like how I feel after I have experienced it.

Alana's Meditation starting technique -

In meditation I find its great to start with a start up technique before I move on to a guided meditation, now this is only what I do and others may do things very differently and that's ok, there is no right or wrong way to do this.

It helps me to feel like I'm protected while meditating, its a very easy technique to try.

Find a quiet place to sit and relax, either in a chair or lean back onto a wall, or you can lay down, I like to lay down somewhere quiet and I always use my headphones when listening to any meditation.

Close your eyes and get comfortable, I then tell my gatekeeper that I'm doing a meditation and I would like her to keep watch for me and only let spirits in that will be there for my highest good from the light only.

Then try and visualise a bright white sparkly light going into your crown on the top of your head, when you breath out imagine the light moving down your head to your neck, breathe slowly and do it in your own time, then move it down into your chest until it gets to your waist, then move it from your shoulders down both your arms until its at the tip of your fingers, then starting at your waist move it down both legs and into your feet, once at the feet then imagine it going through the bottom of your feet and deep into the ground and into a cave that is full of huge crystals and then magnitise the light into the crystal, then I want you to imagine sending all your worries, problems etc right down that light to the crystal and get recycled into pure beautiful energy that is now gold, then send it back up through the ground, up into your feet, then up your legs, and into your hips, up your stomach and chest to your neck, then down your arms and back up again into the neck and up into the head, once at the top of your head push it through your head and out into the sky until you hit the sun, and magnetise the gold light into the sun, and then I like to expand my aura, I imagine the white and gold light that now surrounds me is moving slowly away from my body as long as it feels comfortable, you will know when to stop you will feel it.

Then you are ready to begin your meditations, you can either do this before you start meditating or you can do it during your meditation, but if its a guided meditation you will probably get distracted, so if that is the case just do it before, it will get easier to do with time, but just do it that way for now.

Meditation can be and is practised in many different ways, some do it while driving, some do it in the bath, the shower, the toilet, anywhere where your mind is shut off you are meditating, but there are also many ways you can do it at home.

As I have said before I like to do the guided meditations, but there are many others you can try and you can buy CD's of them, there are DVD's, you can go to a meditation centre, you can do it by yourself or with a group, personally I have tried both.

As a child I had a wonderful teacher, I was in primary school and the teacher was way ahead of her time, she got us to practise breathing methods, meditation, relaxation techniques and she taught us oneness, that we were all one, and that we should all love one another as we would like to be loved, many of the parents were not happy with her teaching us this type of class, but as kids we loved it. Now this is taught in many classes in many schools, and I think that if this type of practise was taught in every school the students would change their thinking, there would be less bullying, more positive outlooks for students and teachers.

I'm so glad I got the opportunity to have that teacher and to be able to have experienced that type of group meditation.

Years later I went to a meditation centre and I experienced another group meditation and although I really enjoyed it, I had decided that for me meditation was best done by myself, less distractions.

These are all your choices so do what is best for you, and what works for you, there are no rules on how you spend your time meditating so just do what makes you comfortable.

There are three primary methods of meditation, so try them out and see what works for you, it you don't like it then try a different one, we are all different so what may work for one, may not work for another.

Focused Attention

These types of meditations are specifically for focusing your attention on one specific thing.

You can focus on a certain object, or your breath, but either way the goal is to concentrate on that one specific thing for the whole time.

Overtime from practise it will become easier and easier to focus, the mind will wander for a while before you get the hang of it, but don't give up, just try a few times a week to get you started or even just for five minutes a day, make it the same time everyday so you can get in the habit of doing it.

Mindfulness

With this kind of meditation you are not focusing on one specific thing, you are letting your mind flow freely without judgement and without attachment.

You are observing your thoughts, memories, your senses, feelings and anything else you pick up while doing it, it allows you to see things from a third person perspective rather from the first person.

You should take note of what your experiencing, and just let it happen, don't judge it, just let it flow and then write it all down at the end of it.

You will generally experience both these practises at the same time, Focused and Mindfulness when you try any of the different types of meditations.

Effortless Transcending

This type of meditation is effortless because you don't need to make an effort or concentrate on anything, it involves emptying your mind, calmness and going inside yourself, this is one of the best ways to meet with your Higher Self because you are leaving your mind open for the interaction.

Your mind becomes so peaceful and open to receive messages from spirit and the feeling you get after your finished is one of pure joy and love.

There are also many various forms of meditations that you can do and use the above techniques in, here a few of my favourites.

Guided Meditations

There are so many different types of guided meditations, you can do them with a specific purpose in mind, like.

- stress relief
- insomnia
- talking with your Angels
- communicating with your Guides
- talking with your Council
- raise your vibration

And many more, so see what works for your needs and try it, there are also many people who post these meditations on utube so start looking, and if you want to communicate with your Angels but the person your listening to doesn't resonate with you then you can find someone else who does the same thing but just a different voice and process.

I like this particular type of meditation not just because it helped to quiet my mind but also I like to listen to someone talking as it gives me something to focus on all the way through, otherwise my mind does wander a lot.

You can also do self hypnosis which is also a form of a guided meditation because you still need to listen to what the person is saying and you will enter a deep state of relaxation, and once you become relaxed, your are more open to the subtle suggestions that are being said throughout the session, and with these you can target certain areas in your life that you would like to change, for example...

- to quit smoking
- to quit drinking
- to change any other habits
- to help with sleep issues
- to open your third eye

Mantra Meditations

This is a Hindu tradition the Mantra Meditations, they involve repeating certain sounds and words with the intention of focusing the mind.

Many different Mantra Schools say that the words and their meanings are very important, but personally I don't think they are, its the intent behind it that is important not the actual word, but that is open to interpretation as many will say different, but again take what resonates with you and throw the rest away, there is no right or wrong, just experience.

As long as you are focusing your attention your intent I don't think you can go wrong.

Many other different religions also use Mantras also but they can also be used if you are not religious, its not primarily for religious purposes.

Personally if I do Mantras I like to do the OM Mantra where I just say OM long and slow, over and over again throughout the meditation, if your interested in doing this type of meditation just look it up on google and choose the one that resonates with you.

Metta Meditations

This type of meditation involves unconditional love and kindness towards other human beings,

It is a compassion meditation and it increases happiness, brainwaves, and neural activity.

Its about love and the goal is to increase good will towards others, and if you first direct love to yourself, you can then direct it to others.

It can really drastically improve your mood over a long period of time.

There are many more different types of meditations and I could go on all day, but to be honest, the only way to find the right one for you is to look for the right one for you, you need to go hunting and find it.

Now I want to talk about the feelings we all get and put down to coincidence, well I'm here to tell you that there are no such things as coincidences, everything happens for a reason.

Do you ever know who is on the other end of the phone when it rings before you even answer it?

Do you ever have a hunch about something and it turns out its true?

Do you ever know that your adult child is not where they say they are, and then you find out you were right?

Have you ever woken up and had a terrible feeling in your stomach and then something horrible happens like you lost a loved one?

Do you ever have a moment where you know that something bad has happened to your child, parent, sibling or friend and then you get a phone call telling you they are sick, or fell out of a tree or they are in hospital?

These are Psychic moments, and so many people dismiss these as coincidences, and they are not, they are a validation that you are in tune with yourself, your loved ones, spirit, the Universe and even Source.

Its what we would call psychic sensing, but most of you would say they were just a hunch, gut instinct, or a sixth sense, but what it really comes down to you being able to pick up psychic information.

Every single person in this world is capable of receiving this information, you just need to know how to do it.

In some way you just need to tune into the frequency, you can strengthen it or not, that is up to you, you can either fine tune it, or you can shut it out, if you believe that you don't have a psychic bone in your body then you wont, if you believe you are capable and would like to give it a try then I say go for it, you will be very surprised.

We are all born with this innate ability and generally by the time we start school and realise its not "normal" to see, hear or feel spirit then we tend to shut it down or turn it off.

Our parents, teachers and other children make us believe that its all rubbish and that we are seeing things that are not there and that if we don't stop talking about it then we will end up in a mental institution.

Its a horrible thing to realise about yourself, that you have this beautiful ability and everyone thinks your nuts.

Over the years things would just pop out of my mouth without me thinking like a friend may have a new man in their life and they ask me what I think of them and all of a sudden I would say, "it wont last, he has a another girl on the side", and I did not even think about it, it just came out, and then I would slap my hand over my mouth wishing I could take it back, and the friend would laugh it off and say whatever, he likes me I know he does, and then a few days later I would get a call from my friend in tears saying her new boyfriend had cheated on her with another girl and she had caught him.

I didn't mean for these things to happen they just happened and sometimes it would make me lose friends because they thought I was weird, or that I could read their minds, and that was creepy to them.

This came from instinct, and my instinct was very strong, it has been all my life, but most of the time I ignored it, and there were times I wish I hadn't but its just they way it was, the way I was.

When I was around eighteen I was outside of my boyfriends house when I heard the sound of a crash, it was a couple of streets away but I knew without a doubt that it was my father in that crash, and although I was in the middle of talking to my boyfriend, I just stopped and turned around and started running towards where the crash had taken place, I just knew where I had to go, and I knew who I would find there, and sure enough when I got there, my father had crashed his car, another car was involved and a policeman was already there.

Psychic Seeing -

Often I would see things out of the corner of my eye, like shadows moving fast or light flashing past my face and then when I have gone to look again and they are gone, do you experience that too?

Do you have dreams that feel so real, that when you wake up you almost freak out that you cant believe that it was a dream all along?

Have you ever been daydreaming and see a scene unfolding like a movie in your head only to shrug it off as a daydream, and then days later you see that exact scene in real life?

If you can relate to any or most of these then its very likely that your dominate clair is clairvoyance – seeing.

The best way to exercise this muscle as such would be to do third eye meditations and exercises, the third eye is located between your eyebrows.

Psychic Feeling -

Have you met someone who automatically got the hairs on the back of your neck standing up?, or have you met someone and instantly knew without a doubt that they will be in your life forever?

This has happened to me every time I meet someone, I will know in that second if they are just going to be aquaintences or if they will be in my life forever, I remember once meeting a girl at my new job and she was giving me the evil eye and her whole body language said back off this is my job, don't step on my toes or I will crush you, but I knew in that instant that she was just being protective and a little scared and that we were going to be very close friends, and 10 years later we still are.

Sometimes my hands get so hot when someone is upset, mad, or extremely sad, really any strong emotion does it to me.

I feel others emotions even before they say a word, and I often take it within me as if its my own, which can really suck sometimes, but there are ways you can control it, which I will get into later.

I feel I can trust someone, not trust someone, know when someone is happy, sad, and all the other emotions like I said.

Have you ever gotten the feeling that someone you loved was in danger?

Have you lost something and then given up finding it, only to just know where it is out of nowhere?

If you can relate to any or most of these then its very likely that your dominate clair is clairsetience – feeling, this is one of the most common of the clairs that people can relate too.

Psychic Hearing -

Have you ever been just hanging around doing whatever you doing to then have someone call your name but your alone in the house?

Have you ever heard beautiful music that sounds far away but close by, but you don't have any music playing?

Do you feel the need to be alone rather than around a lot of people because the noise makes you tired, or gives you a headache, or irritable.

People often don't understand when someone has this ability because they just want you to join in and party with them and all you want to do is to crawl into bed with a book in a quiet room.

Do you have conversations in your head with yourself like all the time?

Would you say your creative, and have ideas to create things often, especially when you are relaxed and feeling grateful?

We often connect to the Source of all things when we are in a quiet place, often that place can be the shower, the toilet, the bath, because we are not thinking of anything, we are in a zen moment of peace, unless your like me and have kids constantly following you into the shower and toilet.

Did you have a "imaginary friend" when you were young? Often these are Angels, loved ones or guides.

Does music make you feel connected? Do you feel your soul being filled with joy, like you have finally found the pieces of your soul, your vibrations is lifted after hearing your favourite music?

Have you been experiencing high pitch sounds in your ears, or like an electrical buzzing in them?

Have you ever been thinking of your grandmother and all of a sudden her favourite song comes on the radio?

If you can relate to any or most of these then its very likely that your dominate clair is clairaudience – hearing.

Psychic Knowing

Have you just had the feeling that you know something, you don't know how, you don't know what makes you think you know but you just know?

Have you ever known that someone was lying to you?, not just because they are good at lying but because you just know they are, this is one of my strongest abilities because I am also an empath too so when someone lies to me I have to learn to pick my battles because sometimes its just not worth the fight.

Do you spend a lot of time writing, or thinking a lot? Do you write music or books, or keep a journal?

Do often get ideas that you cant wait to share, so much so that it will keep you up at night?

Do you just know if someone is trustworthy or not?

Do people always come to you with their questions knowing that you will be able to find the solution?

Do you find it easier to learn through books and writing rather than hearing someone speak?

If you can relate to any or most of these then its very likely that your dominate clair is claircognizance – knowing.

Empathic -

Do you often feel the pain of others?

Do you often feel drained after being around certain types of people for too long?

Do you ever feel sick after being around certain types of people?

Do you ever know when someone says one thing but actually means something else?

Does your mood influence others? Does others moods influence you?

Do people come to you when they have a problem? Do you feel the need to be near water?

Does watching the news or watching violent movie's affect you physically or emotionally?

Do you often care more about others than you do for yourself?

If you can relate to any or most of these then its very likely that your an Empath, often being an empath coincides with being claircognizant.

There are also many different types of Empaths, here are the 6 main types...

An Emotional Empath -

The emotional empath is one of the most common types of empaths, you can easily pick up the emotions of others, and you can also feel those emotions yourself as if they are your own.

Once you work out that it is others emotions and not your own that your experiencing then you can usually just send it away.

Physical / Medical Empath -

You can pick up the energy of other peoples bodies, you can intuitively know what is wrong with the medically, they can also feel them in their own body, which can lead to health problems with themselves.

You can hone this ability by doing some healing training.

Geomantic Empath -

This type of Empathy is related to the physical landscape, you can feel a deep connection to certain places.

You may also be sensitive to the history of the place, and may be able to pick up on sadness, fear or joy that may have occurred over time.

They are highly in tune with the natural world, and grieve any damage that may occur to it.

Spend time in nature.

Plant Empath -

This type of Empath can sense what plants need, you may have a green finger and may have your own beautiful garden at home, some people may receive guidance from tree's and plants/

Spending time with the plants and trees is a must for these empaths and it helps them to attune to them.

Animal Empath -

Many Empaths have a strong connection with animals but an animal empath will devote their life work to them, they may even be able to communicate with animals too.

Many animal empaths also can heal their animals too, as they know what is wrong with them, through communication.

Claircognizant / Intuitive Empath

This type of empath will pick up information from other people just by being around them, you always know when someone is lying, and you can read other peoples energy really well.

They are also able to read others thoughts, and communicate telepathically.

Which Empath do you relate to?

CHAPTER 7

Spirit Communicators

There are many different mediums, psychic's and spirit communicators, they call themselves whatever resonates with them with what they do.

Each medium is different, they communicate with spirits in different ways, I for example am what I choose to call myself an Intuitive Medium, because I feel and know my spirit communication, I also hear spirit in my head, it started off sounding like my own voice, then I started to distinguish between a man and a woman spirit, then I could tell if they were crossed or uncrossed spirits, and now I know who I'm talking to and their name generally, and I can see, hear, feel and know who they are, but when I was still discovering who I was, I found that my clear knowing and clear feeling (Claircognizance and Clairsentient) were my strongest Clairs, so I went with what I knew, but over time, I came to realise that I was more clairvoyant and clairaudient as well, but I decided to keep the name, as it best describes me anyway.

I generally work with your Guides, Angels, and Higher Self as well as your past, present and future lives.

I am not nor have I ever been an evidential medium, and although I will always do my best to relay the information as I get it, although I rarely do your loved ones, but that is only because most people know me as a past life medium so that is where I focus on, but I do on occasion do bring in peoples loved ones.

I would like to show you the different mediums and what they do and how you can choose the right one for you, because by choosing the wrong medium for your needs is like getting a plumber to come bake you some pies, they really are not all the same, so if you are wanting to look for a medium please write down what it is exactly that you are looking to find out from the medium, and then see if what they do matches up with what you want, because many people who go looking for mediums don't choose the right one for their needs and then when they say what they are looking for after the fact its too late, and then often you wont go looking again because you think they are all frauds.

If I had a dollar every time someone said to me, oh I went and saw a psychic and I wanted to talk to my mother in spirit but she just gave me a tarot reading, well then your going to be disappointed, that's not what they do, they are a tarot reader not a medium, unless they do both, which is why you need to find out what it is that they do first before you pay.

Also while we are on the subject I want to touch on paying for a medium, I have seen and heard many people say that what we do is a gift and it should be free and that by charging we are abusing that gift, well let me ask you, do you pay when your favourite singer is singing on stage?, Do you pay for the art that you put on your walls?, Do you pay when you go watch a play?

These are all gifts, singing, art, acting etc and they take time in their lives to do something beautiful for you to enjoy, if you don't like them and don't want to go, then you don't go, you don't stand there at the door telling everyone that its a gift and that it should be free do you?

No so just remember this, if someone is taking time out of their precious life to use their energy to help you then you should expect to pay for that time, just like everything else in this world, nothing comes for free, mediums still have families, they still need to feed them, clothe them etc so don't stand there saying has to be free because its a gift because guess what?, Its not a gift, its an ability, you have it, I have it, everyone has it, we are not special because we are good at it, we just worked harder to use it, and you can too, so if you don't want to see a medium that you have to pay for but you still want answers then guess what, you can have them, you just need to look within to get them, you have the ability too.

This is one of my pet dislikes, I think its very rude for someone to come up to you and say oh you should be spending the three hours it takes you to do a reading and the time away from your family and you should give that to me, I deserve it because you were given that gift as a gift and should be free in return, well guess what, I worked hard to get where I am now, I studied my butt off for a year straight sometimes twelve to fourteen hours a day sometimes longer just so I could be good at it, and to have someone say I don't think I should pay for that is rude and an insult, you would never say that to a trade person who works in your house for half an hour and charges $100, you wouldn't say that to anyone who does a service for you so please don't ask a medium to do it for you.

There are some mediums who agree with that too, and that is totally their choice, they want to spend their energy doing readings for free that is totally their choice.

I admire them, so if you want to get something for free please go look for those people, don't stand on your high horse talking about something you know nothing about judging other people who do, that is your choice, you can be a bully or arm chair warrior or you can just move along and go find someone who can help you and not bully people who wont.

Now on a lighter note, the different types of mediums are very vast so bear with me here, I will do my best to get through as many as I can, but I know there are many others that I don't know about especially because there are many mediums that have multiple abilities so I will do my best.

Psychic Medium

These mediums receive their information via their physical senses, for example the Clairs, as we have talked about before they are :

Clairvoyance – seeing

Clairaudience – hearing

Claircognizance – knowing

Clairsentience – feeling

My strongest abilities are Claircognizance and Clairsentience, but I still have Clairaudience and Clairvoyance which I use for my past life readings, however I also tend to use all four at the same time.

Mediumship

These Mediums talk to spirits in the form of channeling, the information can be received mentally like a form of telepathy, or they can hear the information via Clairaudience.

They can connect to anyone in the spirit world, but not all mediums can see spirit with their physical eyes, more often that not they see it in their minds eye, their third eye.

Again though these mediums can also use all four Clairs to communicate with your loved ones on the otherside.

Medical Intuitive

This type of medium can read your energy and they will receive information about what is going on with your body medically.

They can also most often than not get to the root of what the cause of a physical ailment is.

When looking for this type of medium please always get the advice of a doctor as well, don't use a medical intuitive in place of advice from a medical doctor, always get checked from them as well.

Trance Channeling

This is a type of psychic ability, its where a medium gives permission for a spirit to enter their body, their aura, their headspace etc so that they may talk to the sitter themselves rather than speaking through a third person.

Sometimes the medium is unaware of what has taken place during this time, and sometimes they are well aware, it just depends on how they share the space with the spirit.

The medium is a conduit, however I do not advise anyone try this without another person present, and not until you know what you are doing, seek advice from a trance channeler before even thinking about trying this.

Physical Mediumship

This is something that was popular in the 1800's but the meaning has changed over time in my experience, the original meaning was to get into a deep trance state and allow the spirit to manipulate the energetic matter into the mediums body, the ectoplasm can be maipulated by the spirit to then come out of the mouth or nose of the medium to then project images and or sound.

Table tipping which is also known as table tapping, table turning, or table tilting is also included in physical mediumship, when the spirit can manipulate the table to answer questions.

Its a type of Seance in which people sit around a table, place their hands on it, and wait for rotations. It was found by some scientists over time to be a form of trickery but there are legitimate groups that use this method with success see the book "Doors to past lives & future lives" - practical applications of self hypnosis by Joe H. Slate Ph.D and Carl Llewellyn Weschcke.

It's not something that I recommend but its an interesting read and topic to discuss.

Now a days some people say they are a physical medium meaning an Evidential medium who are there to give evidence that they are talking to who they say they are talking to, which in effect is the same sort of thing, both are a way of giving evidence to the sitter from the spirit, but ill get into that further down.

Mental Telepathy

Is an ability for mediums to communicate through the mind, it can also be known as thought transference and many people have this ability, and many use it to converse with the spirit world, this is also a useful ability for me in knowing what my family is up to.

Evidential Medium

The first thing an evidential medium does is give evidence that the spirit they are conversing with really is your grandmother that passed away five years ago, they will give information like your grandmas favourite flowers, how she died, how old she was when she passed, sometimes they can even get their names, but not always and not all mediums.

Then they will give evidence on what she looked like, what her personality was like, what she liked or disliked and especially anything that stands out about that person when they were in human form, like maybe a limp they had, or a tattoo, or really whatever it is that stands out to the sitter.

The purpose of an evidential reading is to prove that you really are talking to your loved ones and not just some random spirit.

Art Channeler

This type of medium can commune with spirit to create art, they can be accessed in a wide variety of ways, personally I draw what see, so when I'm looking into someone's past life I can see them as if they were standing right in front of me so I can draw a portrait of them, there are many others who can tap into your energy and draw symbols, your soul origin, etc, there are some that will work with your loved one in spirit to paint you a picture from them to you, these are beautiful and I have many friends who are very talented in this area, they are also channeling erik mediums so go take a look under art channelers.

I'm sure there are many more types of mediums out there but like I said these are the ones I deal with on a daily basis and that I'm aware of.

There are many types of services available too, always check with the medium you choose to see what types of services they do before you book.

Past Life and Akashic record reader. Past life drawings

Oracle readings

Psychic medium readings

Art channeling

Distance healing

Physical healing and Reiki Pendulum readings Photo readings

Ribbon readings Tarot readings

Channeling Missing Souls Dream interpretation Palm readers And the list goes on and on, so as long as you know exactly what you want from your reader then you will always get what your looking for, so just take your time when looking for the best medium for your needs, always get a feel for them, do they feel like a good fit?, do you resonate with them?, and were you drawn to them?, sometimes spirit will set it all up before you have even decided that you want to see one, then they will guide you to the right person for your needs.

Past Life Readings

I would like to share with you what I do, how I work, and what a reading with me looks like just to give you a little look into my world with past life readings

This is what a typical reading day looks for me,

12pm – meditate from twenty minutes to an hour depending on how long I feel the reading will go and how much information I need, if I am doing a past life reading it will be twenty minutes of meditation, if I am doing a photo reading and I am talking to a deceased loved one in spirit I may need to do an hour if I feel I haven't had enough time with them.

1pm – I get out my notebook and pen, set up the oracle cards I will be using that day for that reading, at the very least I use two different types, one is the past life cards when I do the past life reading, and the other is the oracle of e deck which I use to help Erik give a little guidance at the bottom of the reading, the cards are a quick way for him to give a little message without doing a full channeling session, and since Erik was the one that help me choose the deck we work with them together, and always have.

I then get my past life crystal when I'm doing a past life reading, which I don't need but I chose to use because it helps me focus on something to empty my mind, then when I'm ready I will ask your higher self or your guides to share with me one of your past lives, if you have never had a reading with me before the first thing I ask for is a life that is affecting this life you are leading right now, if you have already had that life shown to you by me then you can ask for a specific life if you have had a feeling that you have lived a specific one, if not then I will look into another life for you, most of us have lived hundreds and thousands of lives so many people will just keep getting past life readings from me, over and over again, many like to know the lives they have lived.

Then once I have asked for the life they want to share, then I get a movie in my head, I can see you as you were back then, your hair, your body, everything about you, and I see you going about your days, who you talk to etc, but they are only showing me a moment in time because there is a reason why they are showing me this life, they are showing connections with family that you may are still sharing a life with in this life, or they want to show you your death because it may show why you fear certain things in your life now, etc the list goes on, but there is always a reason that they show me what they show me.

I then write it down, everything from your name, your looks if its important, what year or what era it is in, for example they may tell me it was in the early 1700's, where you live at that time, they usually tell me the country, sometimes if its important they will tell me the state, just depends what they want you to know, then once its all written down, then I ask your guides, angels, higherself or loved ones if any of them have a message for you, sometimes that may be a channeled message from them and sometimes they will ask me to pull three cards from the Ask Your Guides Oracle Deck, then I will pull a past life card, sometimes it will relate to the life I just read and sometimes it relates to another life, which you may choose to look at next time.

Last but not least, I will ask Erik if he has a message for you, and if he says yes then I will with his help pull a card from the oracle of e deck, and the message is always profound if only short.

So this is how I work, I like it to be very quiet when I work, it helps me see better and get better information for the sitter, I am also working on a one on one session with mediumship which my circle and I have been doing for months now, twice a week, every week, just to practise and although I believe my mediumship is coming along nicely, I know I'm not ready to do be doing it yet as a paid service, not because I can't but because I don't have the same confidence in it as I do with my private email readings, it is just what works for me at this time.

One day I will add skype one on one readings to my services but not in the near future.

I want to share one of the past life readings I did for a client so you can see what a reading from me looks like, to protect the clients identity I have changed their name and I have left out some personal parts of the reading.

I have also not added the cards to the reading here either as they are personal to the client as well.

Past Life Reading by Alana

Rebecca I see you as a young girl in the 1700's. Your family is what I guess you would call middle class, your comfortable and don't "Need or Want" for anything in this life. Your father has a very good job and he supports you and your mother quite comfortably.

Your name is Katherine and you are twelve years old.

You and your mother butt heads daily as you at the stage of not quite a teenager and yet not quite a little girl any more, and you feel you should be given more freedom to go out with your friends without a chaperone, and your mother still insists that for your own protection and because that was just the way things were, that you must still continue to have one.

Your father isn't any help either as he says its your mothers decision as she is the one in charge of you and so he says just be a good girl and do what your mother says.

However you are starting to hate her and her rules.

One day you decided you had had enough of your parents rules and you packed up some clothes and you decided to move in with your friend Emma's family (although you hadn't actually asked them, you were just under the impression they would let you).

So while your mother was out on errands you left to go on the long walk there, its about a thirty minute horse and carriage ride there normally so you weren't aware that it may be much longer by foot, but off you went and by this stage it had started to snow so you started to worry a little but you were determined to leave so you ignored it.

When your mother got home and realised you were not home where she had left you in the hands of the housekeeper/nurse who was supposed to be watching you (you had snuck past her), then she started to panic, but she had to wait for your father to get home before anything could be done, and once he did he went out and looked for you.

When they hadn't found you a few hours later they were forced to wait until morning to resume the search.

They found your body two days later, you had gotten lost and taken shelter under a tree overnight, but by the time they had found you, you were frozen solid and had died of heart failure due to hypothermia.

Your parents were heartbroken because by this stage they had realised that you were running away and it broke their heart.

I feel I was shown this life in particular because you will be going through this struggle soon if you aren't already, the tween age can be a struggle and your guides are saying that nothing like that will ever happen again.

So as you can see I will also connect the life with the life they are living now if its connected.

The reading is very detailed and very long, but like I said I am only showing you the past life reading part of it for privacy reasons.

Many past life readers also do their readings differently too, so its very rare to find two people who work exactly the same in the same area.

So go get yourself a past life reading and see what your past shows you, you may be very surprised what you can learn about yourself from a past life reading.

CHAPTER 8

Sign's your loved ones are around

There are many signs that your loved ones are around you, I have spent my life experiencing many before I even realised what they were or what they meant, so I wanted to let you know that your not alone, a lot of people experience these signs and they just brush them off as weird, which is what I did growing up, but once you know what to look for you can also communicate with your loved ones too.

This is not something that is for mediums alone anyone can experience signs every single person in the world can.

Smelling perfume, tobacco, flowers and any other abnormal smell.

Have you ever been sitting in a room where you were just relaxing in front of the TV and all of a sudden you smell flowers, or freshly baked bread for example and thought wow that reminds me of grandma, she loved those flowers or she used to love baking fresh bread, there is a very good chance that was your grandma letting you know she is around, this is one way our loved ones let us know that they are still around and they still love you, even if you weren't close to them in life.

Like my own grandmother for example, which who I have already mentioned, we were not close in life but now we are as close as two people could be, she is my gatekeeper, my strength and my protector, not to mention my Grams.

So don't ignore those signs, they are saying they love you, so tell them back and say thankyou to them for visiting you.

These smells can seriously be anything, even down to dirty smelly socks, Erik loves to bombard us with those kind of smells, its his way of letting you know its him, those and fart smells are his favourite.

Erik literally bombarded me with that smell for months until I finally figured it out it was him and then it went away, I rarely smell it now because I know when he is here, where as I didn't before.

I have also smelled perfume, a roast cooking, chocolate, beer, tobacco pipe, and even cigarette smoke, there are many more smells you just need to figure out where they connect with your loved ones.

So if you find your smelling a smell that's out of place where you are, know that its your loved ones saying hi, I miss you and I love you.

Dream Visitations

Have you lost someone close to you, and then had a dream about them?, Did you think wow that was weird, must be my subconscious messing with me?

Well its not, this is the easiest way for our loved ones to communicate with us, when our bodies and minds are at rest.

They often won't say anything with their mouths but will talk to us telepathically, as this is how they talk in spirit, mind to mind, so don't freak out when you hear them but their mouths are not moving, this is normal.

They want to let you know that they aren't dead, they have just changed forms, and this is the easiest way for them to achieve that.

Finding coins and feathers

Have you ever found a feather on your pillow, or in your path, or been walking around only to find a coin in your path or in your house that had no way of getting there?

These are signs that your loved ones are around, they will put them in your path so only you will find it, they spend time watching and waiting for the right moment to place it in your path, its not an easy task for them as they want you to know that its from them, and most of the time it gets brushed off as a coincidence so take note.

When you find a feather, check out the colours ad then look online and see what the colours mean, they all have meaning and this is how they communicate with you, and its also a good reminder to pay attention to your surroundings, your thoughts etc as our thoughts can be very powerful.

When your thinking bad things about yourself and others it can manifest bad things happening over and over again.

When you start to think good thoughts, you will start to manifest good things happening in your life, so watch what you think.

For example some feather colour meanings are -

White – Spirituality, have faith, you are protected, hope and your angels
   are near.
Blue – Peace, spirit connection, psychic awareness and inspiration.
   Orange – Change is coming, energy, success and love.
Red – Good fortune, emotions, courage, security, money and passion.
Yellow – Mental alertness, joy, vision, cheerfulness and intelligence.
Green – health, healing, nature, prosperity, success and nature spirits.
Black – Protection, warning and mystical wisdom.
Pink – Unconditional love, romance, compassion, honour, inspiration
   and harmony.
Grey – Peace and neutrality.

Brown – Stability, grounding, friendship, home, endurance and respect.

These and many more can be found on many websites, along with other colours and other meanings.

I suggest www.in5d.com for all your meaning needs.

Angel Numbers

This is one of the most common ways our angels, guides, higher selves ad loved ones to get our attention.

They will put recurring numbers in our path, so you may start off looking at the clock and seeing 11.11am for example, and then go to the shops and get a receipt which says you spent $11.11 or your docket number might be 1111, then you may be driving home and see a cars number plate with 1111, so you get the picture, they will be everywhere.

This was the first time I realised about angel numbers, when I was constantly seeing 11.11 or 1.11 and then overtime I began to see 2.22, 3.33, 4.44 etc repeatedly, and now I see 5.11,7.11 and 9.11.

They all have meaning, so when you see this recurring in your daily life take note, look up the numbers you are seeing, this is the beginning of your awakening as such, this is when your spiritual path has begun.

The best website I have found for looking up accurate angel numbers is on www.joannesacredscribe.com and I only refer her to anyone that wants to look up their own numbers.

For example from her site what 11.11 means....

Many people associate the repeating numbers 1111 with a wake up call, a code of activation, or awakening code.

It can also be seen as a key to unlock the subconscious mind, and reminds us that we are spiritual beings having a physical experience rather than physical beings embarking upon spiritual experiences.

Upon noticing a frequency of 1111's appearing repeatedly, you may begin to see an increase in synchronicities and unlikely and miraculous coincidences appearing in your life.

At time when you are about to go through a major ritual wakening or an epiphany of some kind, the number 1111 may appear in your physical reality and experience to signal the upcoming change or shift.

When noticing the angel numbers 1111 appearing, take note of the thoughts you had right at that moment, as 1111 indicates that your thoughts and beliefs are aligned with your truths.

For example, if you help an inspired idea at the time of seeing 1111, it would indicate that it would be a positive and productive idea to take action on.

When angel number 1111 appears repeatedly, it signifies that an energetic gateway has opened up for you, and this will rapidly manifest your thoughts into realities.

The message is to choose your thoughts wisely, ensuring that they match your true desires.

Do not put your energy into focusing on fears as you may manifest the in your life.

(Taken from Joanne's website, she has all the numbers on there so go take a look)

I agree with the last part about not putting energy into your fears, when you focus on fear, or the things that make you fearful, you can manifest fearful things for real, so keep your thoughts on good things, pleasant things.

Objects being moved

You swear you put that object down in one place and then you find it somewhere else and no one else is home, so how did it move?, or are you going crazy?

Well no your not going crazy, unless you are of course and then that is a whole other story.

Well your loved ones will try and get your attention whenever possible, they may put an object that means a lot to you because it belongs to said loved one and they want to let you know they are there so they will move it to get your attention.

They will also do it just to get your attention so you can say hey I know I left that there, so where is it gone?, then you will ask someone about it and that may lead you to finding out more, there is a method to their madness of making us feel crazy.

Sensing / feeling your loved ones

When you have lost someone who you knew very well in life like a parent, sibling etc you know its them when they are standing next to you, you just know, well when they cross over they know you can feel them, so they will come to you often to let you know they are there.

Music

Do you often get in the car and there will be a song on the radio that reminds you of that special someone who has passed?

They will often manipulate electronics to makes you hear that song at that exact time, for example if I'm feeling down and I go for a drive, I guarantee my grandma will put on the song Hello by Adele, that is or song, and when I go to a fish and chip shop for lunch or dinner every time, every single time Erik will put on the song I come from a land down under by men at work, this is our song.

So just keep your ears and your mind open and watch how many times a certain song comes on, especially when your thinking about your loved ones.

Electrical Activity

You may find your light globes blowing, or your lights flickering, computer not working properly, emails disappearing, the phone ringing and no one is at the other end and many other electrical phenomenon.

These again are your loved ones letting you know they are there, I have even seen spirits post on their own facebook page that no one else has access to even after its been memorialised.

Being Touched by spirit.

This one can frighten people, but honestly there is nothing to be frightened of, they sometimes will touch your face because they want to feel your energy, and sometimes you will feel that, many times everyday I feel as though someone has their hand around my upper left arm, its my grandmother, as soon as I acknowledge her the feeling goes away.

So just say hi, I feel you ad thankyou and it will go away, don't ever be frightened, keep your thoughts pure with only love not fear, and your will enjoy the experience, and they will be able to do it more often for you they need to try and match our lower vibration ad that is not easy, so its easier to keep love in or hearts and minds to match their vibration instead, and then we will experience more and more.

Most asked Question's and Answer's

Question - How can we get a message from the universe regarding or path?

Answer – There are many ways we can find our own answer regarding our path, and the best way I know how is either speak directly to your guides via automatic writing, or I like to just ask my guides directly, I say ok send me a song that will let me know if I am on the right path, or if I'm not on the right path please send me a song that will lead me onto the right path.

When I asked this question myself not that long ago the song I received was Katy Perry – Firework.

You should sit quietly and ask the question you want answered and the first song to pop in your head is the answer, then go look up the lyrics and see what they are saying about your path.

Question – I would like to know how to deal with loved ones who are religious and that think our abilities are evil.

Answer – Yes this can be a difficult one, it really depends on the person your talking to and their belief system and if they are willing to let you have your opinion and they keep theirs to themselves.

If they are not going to let it go, then you may need to make a choice, is it worth it to listen to them say horrible things about you and just ignore it?, or do you think you may need to walk away from them?

That is only a question that you can answer for yourself, but my advice is be kind to yourself and respect yourself enough that your not going to let people be nasty to you, decide if your ready to let these people go, and they may be your parents, your siblings, etc but is it worth it to be picked on daily?

Now I'm only asking adults this question not children, because unfortunately you don't get to have a say on whether you want them out of your life or not, so you need to wait until you can, but always try and work things out if you can.

Question – Is it true that when you cross over you get a life review?, and what is it about?

Answer – Yes its true that most people when they cross over will get a life review, some don't need them because they are more of an evolved soul and they remember everything when they cross over, so they don't need to, however some may choose not to have their review's straight away, they may decide to rest for a while, they can pretty much do whatever they want when they cross over, including to come and hang out with their family here for a while, if that is what they choose.

What I have been told by spirits, well those that have had the review has said its just a big movie of your life, you get to see what you accomplished, what you didn't, if you want to do it again to achieve those goals, or if you want to achieve it where they are.

There is no right or wrong with your life review, your not judged except maybe by yourself, but you are the only person that will, its all just a learning experience, not a judgement hangout.

Question – How do spirits know who to go to to get heard, how do they know we are mediums, lightworkers etc, how do they see us?

Answer – Well when I have asked this question myself I was told that we have bright lights of auras coming off us that they can see, they say that when we evolve in our spirituality our lights get brighter so we are easier to see and its easier for them to connect to us.

Question – Will we be able to eat, drink etc when we cross over?

Answer – Not physically no but we can experience it yes, its just not the same experience as it is as being a human.

But they can certainly manifest whatever they want, they want their house they had at home?, no problem there it is, you want pizza?, there it is, so the answer is yes and no, because after a while you wont need these human things, its more of a comfort until you are used to not having that human need anymore.

Question – How does spirit help to clarify thoughts and feelings which people were unsure or confused about?

Answer – There are many ways spirit can help to clarify your thoughts and feelings especially if they are not your own, if by chance your an empath, you will often find you have thoughts in your head or feelings that you feel that you may think wait what, I'm not feeling this way so where is it coming from, so you suddenly feel angry, sad, happy, in love, then you hear the neighbours fighting, or there is a girl walking past the house crying.

I always look to myself first, then if I know that it isn't my feelings I'm feeling I will look to the people in the house at the time, if they aren't feeling it, then I look outside the house, and if there is a girl walking past crying then I know I'm picking up on her feelings.

If you have suddenly become angry all the time, to the point you start being destructive with yourself, eg, start taking drugs, or drinking alcohol a lot then I would start looking at where things took a turn for the worse, did it just start happening?

Has it been happening for a long time?

If you say yes then I would start by seeing a doctor, then a medium, especially a past life medium as it may be past life related, or it may be part of your contract to experience it, so find out if it is part of what you are meant to go through, because it may help to know what is what, and then the medium can also suggest where to go next for help.

I want to make it very clear though, always see a doctor first and foremost, if they can eliminate anything health related and this goes for any of the symptoms or habits etc then let them, and then see a medium.

You don't ever want to mess around with your health, I always get the doctor to check first and then look for other avenues.

Question – Do animals go to heaven or is there a different heaven for them?

Answer – Absolutely they go where everyone else goes, animals are highly intuitive and are excellent companions, they generally will wait for you for when you pass, and they may choose to stay as animals or they may turn into the original being they are, my cat for example decided to go back to his alien form, he came to the earth to see what human love was like, we spent sixteen years together, I talked about him at the very beginning his name was Mia.

I was there when he died and it was the worst day of my life, but as an adult I found out what his purpose was and was able to communicate with him myself, it was very strange watching him go from a cat to a alien.

Yes I know sounds like the weirdest thing you have ever heard? Well imagine watching it.

Question – Do soul groups really exist?

Answer – Of course, we are all part of a soul group, there a very close soul groups also known as inner soul groups, outer soul groups and I'm sure there are many more different soul groups but these are the only ones I know about at this stage because I know who are in those groups from my family, like I mentioned before my husband is from my outer soul group, so is one of my children, and the others are in my inner soul group. I know also that some of my very close friends are from my inner soul group too, even some that I have never met in person, who I am very close with, so look at your friends and family and ask yourself who they are in your soul group and listen to what your instinct tells you, you may be surprised at what you learn.

I have even found friends who I have never met who have been in my past life together with me, I have found sisters, parents and even very close friends that I lived with in a past life.

Question – Do you remember any of your past lives and deaths?

Answer – Of course I remember many of my own past lives, in one I was a medicine man, in another I was murdered by my husband along with my child, we were pushed off a cliff while hiking, and another life I fell out of a tree when I was 8 years old, and in another I fell off the roof of my house, I was with my twin sister (who is now a male friend of mine in this life) and we were hiding from men who looked like bandits, they were coming to take something from us (our supplies I believe) and our big sister told us to hide because they were dangerous men.

111

She told me to go out the window on the second story roof and wait until they had gone, my twin hid under the bed as she was afraid of heights but I went on the roof, and I was curious about who the men were and I leaned over to look around the corner to look at their horses and to see if they were going yet and I fell, I fell and broke my neck.

I remember many of my past lives and many of my past deaths, sometimes it can be useful to know who you were and how you died, because sometimes we bring these worries into our current lives, I had a fear of flying for years and once I found out why I had that fear I no longer had such a great fear, I have been able to control it with the help of my angels and guides.

So if you have a fear then ask your guides to let you see the past life that is affecting you in this life, and then either meditate on it or ask it to come into a dream, or you can book in with a past life regressionist to help you find out, or you can book in with a past life reader like myself, or a Akashic records reader, any of these can help you find out what you need to know, but first I suggest trying to find out on your own, you have the power to do all that I have suggested in this book, everyone is able to tap into this knowledge.

Every single person has this knowledge available to them.

Question – When you get a message from spirit how do you know if it is for you, or if its for someone else, and how do you know what the message is?

Answer – Messages can come in many shapes and forms depending on the ability the person has, sometimes it can come in symbols, hearing the message, seeing the message in the form of pictures, or you may get it telepathically, or you may just hear a song, so how do you know if its for you or someone else?

Well quite often messages are like jigsaw puzzles, and we need to put all the pieces together, like for example I may get a smell first, then a song, then words, then hearing certain messages sometimes I get the whole message and I instantly know who its for and what its about, and sometimes it takes me days to figure it out, like the Peter Allan message.

Generally though I get told the message is for a certain person, and then I get the message and then I decide whether or not I will relay this message to the person.

Sometimes I know its not going to be received well, and sometimes I know it will be received fine, it just depends, so go with your instincts, if it says no don't do it, then don't, if it says yes go ahead then do it, but ultimately it comes down to you, if you want to or not, not everyone is keen on giving messages when they come, so feel its not ethical, some just don't like doing it unless the person the message for has book an appointment with them because it could upset the person, for me I honestly don't mind, if a message comes through then if I feel its ok to go ahead and give it, if I don't think it will be ok I wont.

Songs have the best messages if your just beginning to get messages that your noticing, it may be a song your loved one loved in life, or it may be one that has a message in it for you.

Symbols are not something I get often but some people only get them or they get them as well as other symbols.

Always listen to your instinct on who the message is for, it will never steer you wrong, and then ask what the message is, if your not getting enough information to be able to give a message then ask for more, they will always give you more, so just keep your eyes out for them.

How symbols that can come through are...

- Seeing symbols
- Hearing symbols
- Feeling symbols
- Smelling and tasting symbols

Seeing symbols

You may see flashes of colours, or images through your third eye, they may look like movies, photographs and they can be anything from something small or they can be extremely detailed.

Hearing symbols

You may experience your sixth sense when you hear a song or a tune in your head, sometimes you may get a name, many people feel like they are making it up because they hear it in their own voice to start with, sometimes they may only hear it in their own voice so it seems like it may be your own thoughts and not from a spirit.

Feeling symbols

Feeling symbols can be quite tricky for some, as you may get a feeling of a headache for example and it may mean you have picked up on a tumour or a problem with the head, you may get a feeling of floating in water which may make you feel sick which may represent the person your reading for may be feeling nauseated.

There are many ways to interpret so its a matter of finding what works for you, this is where writing down what you see will help when you get the same feeling again down the track, and you can refer to your notes to put the pieces together

Smelling and Tasting symbols

If you are smelling cigars for example and no one is in the house, you can either interpret it as a person or loved one you knew who smoked in life, or you may interpret it differently, its just a matter of figuring out what it means to you.

Some symbols you may see and their meanings …

Animals – natural instinct, or instinctive decisions. Apple - represents the need for healthy eating. Angels – help is there for you, just need to ask.

Baby – you may be pregnant or someone close to you may be pregnant or needing to explore your inner child.

Bag – life experiences, responsibilities, or burdens we carry.

Bath – sign of emotions, the need to spiritually clean, can also represent feeling emotionally drained.

Battery – a need to recharge, rest and rejuvenate.

Bed – time to rest, sleep and may also represent sexual relationships.

Birds – time to spread your wings and fly, take a journey or freedom.

Boat – vacation, cruise, or can represent a journey through life.

Birthday cake – message from your family on the other side saying happy birthday, or someone else's birthday.

Books – research, wisdom, information or school.

Boy – To stop being childish, or childish behaviour with someone else, may refer to sports, or may be specifically related to a boy.

Girl – new ideas, a new birth, may be specifically related to a girl.

Dragonflies – spirituality, a connection with spirit, message from spirit.

Butterfly – beauty, transformation, freedom, or a sign from a spirit

There are so many different meanings for so many different things so if your wanting to look further into this google the meanings or there are many books that will help you to discover the meanings, or go within and ask your spirit team what they mean and listen to what they have to say, like I have said before their messages to you can come in many different forms, you just have to know how and when to read the signs, but make it simple, ask if the answer to your question is yes then you want to see a butterfly, if its no then you want to see a feather in your path, there are many ways we can get these question's answered.

AFTERWORD

Love and guidance will always be available with spirit, they are there for you, even when you are not there for yourself, they will never ever give up on you, no matter what, and you are never alone, you are the most important people in the world to your loved ones and guides.

Anytime you are feeling alone or lonely, just know that spirit is right there with you feeling it with you, and trying to find ways to let you know that you are not alone.

The second you think of your loved ones is the second they are by your side, so when people ask me to please send a message to Aunt Jo or Grandma etc they already did themselves the second they thought of them, I always tell people that they already did send it, they hear you, they know you, they feel you, and most of all they love you.

And I love you too, no matter who you are, how you live, or what you do, we are one, the whole world and its people are one, whenever someone asks about us being one I always remind them of the song by The Seekers called "We are Australian"

Here are the lyrics for you, enjoy and never forget, no matter what, where, how or why, we are one and always will be.

We Are Australian
We are one, and we are many
And from all the lands on earth we come,
We'll share a dream and sing with one voice
I am, you are, we are Australian.

Have a listen to the song, its a great song and its personally one of my favourite Australian songs, but it shows that we are one, and although they are mostly talking about Australians, it also talks about all the lands on earth we come, and we sing with one voice.

What I am saying is, talk to people, actually listen to them, people from all walks of life are fascinating, and you don't know someone's story or walked in their shoe's, so you don't know them, don't listen to other peoples opinion of others, find out for yourself, if I had have listened to others first when I had met my best friend then I would have missed out on a awesome chick, when you listen to others, you are missing out of finding things out for yourself and what works for one person, may not work for another.

So don't rob yourself of an experience that you may have because of someone else, take charge and work things out for yourself, I would have missed out of ten years of so much fun if we had both listened to others about each other, there were people that didn't think we would like one another, so they tried very hard to stop us from being friends, but boy were they wrong, and ten years later we are still going strong, so do yourself a favour and listen to your own instincts, not anyone else's.

Printed in the United States
By Bookmasters